# The Power of Personality

- UNLEASH YOUR POTENTIAL IN ALL THAT YOU DO -

Cover illustration provided by Christian Bilbow

First published in Great Britain in 2015 by
Customer Psychology ltd.
Oxford

ISBN 978-1508590460

# The Power of Personality

- UNLEASH YOUR POTENTIAL IN ALL THAT YOU DO -

Gareth English

With Angelina Bennet, Linn Brynildsen, Bernard Cooke, Anna Crollick, Natasha Graham, Rachael Lewis, Pauline Siddons and Rob Toomey.

# :: Contents ::

# :: About the Author ::

Gareth English is a Psychologist and Director at Customer Psychology Ltd. He has worked for over 15 years as a business consultant, specialising in understanding the role that personality plays in our lives.

Gareth worked for a number of consultancy companies before co-founding Customer Psychology in 2010, with the goal of applying the principles of personality assessment and understanding to clients, stakeholders and customers.

He is the creator of the Type Accelerator, An online tool to help people to get more from Personality Type.

Whilst he enjoys building the business, investigating new technologies and conducting research, what he still loves most of all are those simple lightbulb moments when a single person sees themselves in a new way.

# :: Introduction

The purpose of this book is to provide readers with new ways to look at and consider Personality Type.

As a psychologist I'm interested in understanding the human mind and personality questionnaires are a way of doing just that. There are loads of options out there and I've worked with a great many of them. So why choose the idea of Personality Types? Since I'm specifically a business psychologist I'm interested in the application of psychology. So I'm constantly looking to balance the quality of ideas with their applicability. Ideally, of course, I like ideas that are high in quality and also easy to apply. That's why I use the Type approach. After over 15 years working as a psychologist, with various models, I've found that it is the most effective approach for clients to help them understand themselves and others. There are other models of personality that I've used. Some of these appeal to me as a psychologist because they can try to account for everything a person might do. Unfortunately, though, they often end up so complicated that it's hard for my clients to get to really get to the value.

Any tool is only as good as its application. And Personality Type tools are just the same. It's one thing to have some useful knowledge about how people are different, but that knowledge only really helps us if we are able to put it into practice. So the intention of this book is to help you to get more from Psychological Type.

I've gathered together people who apply Personality Type in a variety of ways, from team building and coaching to parenting and exercise. What they all have in common is their level of experience. Each has at least a decade of experience in applying Personality Type. Each has worked with hundreds of individuals. So another way of looking at this is that this book contains over 100 years of experience, gathered through helping thousands of people not just to learn about Type, but to apply it. So now here they all are, together in this book, to share their learning with you.

For those who are already practised users of Personality Type, we hope to give you some new tips and techniques from the decades of experience amongst our experts. We may even open your mind to some areas where you hadn't yet applied Type to your work or to the rest of your life.

For those of you who are new to the idea of Personality Type, I hope that this book will serve as an introduction to a fascinating way to understand yourself and others. You will certainly find a massive range of opportunities to apply your new understanding of yourself and other people.

## Getting the most from this book

Since there are likely to be different people reading this book I thought I'd add a few thoughts about where to start.

### Type experts

Personality Type is all very familiar to you and you're looking to get some new, deeper insights. If you haven't already done so then I suggest you take a look at the Table of Contents and find the topics that look the most interesting. The chapters towards the back of the book are generally those that work with concepts like Type Dynamics.

### Familiar with Type

You've come across Personality Type before and you're quite familiar with your own Type, but you wouldn't consider yourself an expert. The first few chapters of this book have the most straightforward applications of Type, so that might be a good place to start. Once you're back into the swing of it then the later chapters, which require a bit more understanding of Type in depth, will make more sense.

If you would like to take a look, the rest of this introductory chapter has a refresher on the basics of Personality Type.

## New to Personality Type

Welcome!

If you really want to gain a thorough understanding of Type then you should go for 'interactive feedback.' That involves completing a questionnaire and then working through that with someone who is trained in interpreting the results and giving feedback. That may sound daunting – but the results can be amazing. There are loads of ways of doing this – the most widely known is the Myers-Briggs Type Indicator® (or MBTI®), although there are lots of other great options. There are also free resources on the internet that will offer a personality questionnaire. What they're often missing out on, though, is the interactive feedback. This doesn't have to be face to face—some products like TypeCoach® do this very well using technology but, for me, something to stretch your thinking is a must. Great interactive feedback lets you really understand what this all means for you—it will challenge you to think about how you can put it into practice and what you will do differently as a result of what you've learnt.

So maybe put 'get interactive feedback' on your to-do list, then have a look at the rest of this chapter which is a brief introduction to the ideas of Personality Type. Once you have that under your belt you can tackle the rest of the book. As you work through it you will build up your understanding of the ways that Personality Type can be used to analyse a whole range of situations, like shopping, coaching, parenting and exercising. And when you go for that interactive feedback you'll have a better understanding of the ways that your behaviour is determined by Personality Type.

---

* MBTI, the MBTI logo, Myers-Briggs Type Indicator and Myers-Briggs are registered trade marks of the Myers & Briggs Foundation. OPP Ltd is licensed to use the trade marks in Europe.

# An introduction to Personality Types

The way we think about Personality Type today largely comes from the work of a Swiss psychiatrist called Carl Jung, who found systematic differences in the way people think. Of course this wasn't the first time that anyone had come across this idea and Jung was building on the work of many thinkers, philosophers and scientists who had come before him. However, he did put it in terms that made a lot of sense to a lot of people.

## Different Types of people

Jung's work has been built on in the last hundred years or so and today there are loads of different ways of measuring Personality Type, with researchers like Myers and Briggs or Kiersey and Bates being highly influential.

Jungian Personality Types identify four important choices. Making a choice on each of these options will give you a 'four-letter' Type, for example, ESTJ. More about this in a few moments, but first – five things that you should know about Personality Types.

*1.  It's not about how much*
You're one thing or another. That's your Type preference. When people talk about 'how much', they mean your behaviour, which is slightly different. You have a preference for one or the other. Simple. That's your Personality Type. Your behaviour is a more complicated mixture.

*2.  It's not about how good you are*
I like singing in the shower. My singing is terrible. What you prefer is not necessarily the same as what you're great at.

*3.  Everyone does all of them*
This is really key. Everyone uses all of the Type preferences every single day. We all do some things in our inner world and some things in the outer world. We look at some details, we look at some patterns. But we find one of each of those options easier. That's our preference.

*4. It's not about being put in a box*
Your Personality Type is your favourite room in a house. You can go into any of the other rooms, but this one is your favourite.

*5. You can change your mind*
If you get to know yourself better, you may decide that you've changed your mind about who you really are. The more you know about yourself and the more you know about Type, the more you may increase your understanding of who you were all along. This is, of course, why good interactive feedback is the key to getting the most from Type.

• • • • • • • • • • • • • • • •

So what are these choices? Well, they concern four key areas of how you use your mind.

1. Where do you get your energy?
2. What information do you trust?
3. How do you make decisions?
4. How do you live your life?

## 1. Extraversion or Introversion – It's all about energy

This is an easy one to get confused about as the words are used in lots of different contexts nowadays. However, what we're talking about here is where you get your energy from.

People who prefer Introversion get energised from their inner world. Reflecting, focusing, spending time by themselves or with very close friends, these are the things that energise them. We use the letter I to refer to this, as Introversion is a long word to keep writing and saying.

People who prefer Extraversion get energised by interacting with the outer world. Talking, doing, action, these are the things that energise them. We use the letter E to refer to this.

People who prefer *Extraversion* tend to:

- Get energised interacting with people
- Learn by doing
- Tend to have a breadth of interests
- Lose energy if they have to focus on one thing by themselves
- Like to speak up quickly in meetings.

People who prefer *Introversion* tend to:

- Get energised focusing and reflecting
- Learn by thinking
- Tend to have fewer interests, which they really get into
- Lose energy if they have to interact with a lot of new people
- Like to consider what they will say before speaking up in a meeting.

## 2. Sensing or iNtuition – What information do you trust?

This preference pair is simply about how we take in information. What information do you trust the most? Some people look for real, practical, detailed information. Others look for meaning, associations and trusted patterns.

We call preferring the detailed, specific information Sensing and we use the letter 'S'. We call preferring the meaning and associations iNtuition and we use the letter 'N' (we've used up the letter I already with Introversion).

This affects everything – from the instructions that we like, to the books and films we prefer, and even the way that we speak. Those who prefer S tend to be more direct and say what they mean, while those who prefer N are more likely to use metaphors and analogies.

People who prefer *Sensing* are:

- Grounded in reality
- Excited by what is real and actual
- Trust what they can see and touch
- Need to see specific details before they can get their head around the bigger picture.

People who prefer *iNtuition* are:

- Focused on the future
- Excited by possibilities
- Trust their insights
- Need to see the bigger picture before they can get their head around the details

## 3. Thinking or Feeling – How do you make decisions?

If S-N is about information, then Thinking-Feeling is about how you make decisions based on that information. Everyone makes decisions all the time, but when you're making them, does your head rule your heart or your heart rule your head?

If you let your head make decisions because you like logic and objectivity, we call that Thinking, and use the letter T. If your heart rules your head because values and harmony are more important to you then we call that Feeling, and we use the letter F.

### Some misconceptions

Because harmony is important to them, some people think that F folks are just soft and fluffy. This can be true. If you treat them honestly and sincerely they will value you and the relationship they have with you. But if you think they're a pushover then you've never seen an F stand up for what they believe in.

Because they value logic and objectivity, some people think that Ts are cold and uncaring. They love their families, they love their friends, they love their cats, dogs or iguana. But when they are making decisions they try to put aside their emotions to be objective.

Those who prefer *Thinking* tend to:

- Look for cause and effect reasoning
- Easily see flaws – what could be done better
- Use the phrase "I think..."
- Try to be as objective and logical as possible.

Those who prefer *Feeling* tend to:

- Try to live in harmony with the people around them
- Easily see strengths – what went well
- Use the phrase 'I feel...'
- Try to treat people as individuals as far as possible.

### 4. Judging or Perceiving – How do you deal with the world around you?

The Americans use a great word – closure. That's just what this preference pair is all about.

Some people like closure. They like to have things decided, sorted and done. We call this Judging, and we use the letter J. Other people like to keep their options open – why commit to something before you have to? We call this Perceiving, and we use the letter P.

People who prefer Judging like closure. People who prefer Perceiving dislike closure.

#### At work
This is a tricky one at work. Being a manager, looking after projects, working in a large organisation, these can all include having to do

lots of J stuff, like making decisions and plans. So keep an eye out for whether you really like closure, or if this is just something you've learnt to do for your job.

People who prefer *Judging*:

- Enjoy closure
- Like to have things decided and sorted
- Feel less comfortable with ambiguity
- Don't like last-minute rushes.

People who prefer *Perceiving*:

- Like to decide things when they *have* to
- Enjoy looking at the different options
- Find ambiguity interesting
- Often find a last-minute rush exhilarating.

## More than the sum of the parts

Like a chemical formula (or a cocktail if that suits your lifestyle!), the sum of the parts says much more. Rather than thinking of these as four separate choices, instead you can think of the choices as the code that unlocks your four-letter Personality Type. This is generally referred to as 'whole Type'.

Once you have that code then you can tell a lot more about yourself than just what you answered to the individual preferences.

Unfortunately, I don't have the space here to write a great deal about each of the 16 preferences. But, as you will see, the other chapters of this book will reference this whole Type (or parts of it) to relate to how you apply Type to a range of situations. After all that's the power of personality.

Here is a short flavour of each of the whole Types:

ISTJ: Hard-working and considerate
ISFJ: Conscientious and loyal
INFJ: Thoughtful and reflective
INTJ: Ingenious deep thinkers
ISTP: Realistic specialists
ISFP: Considerate and grounded
INFP: Deep and principled
INTP: Curious problem-solvers
ESTP: Resourceful and adaptable
ESFP: Friendly and flexible
ENFP: Playful and original
ENTP: Quick-thinking and challenging
ESTJ: Action-oriented fixers
ESFJ: Friendly and practical
ENFJ: Idealistic and harmonising
ENTJ: Visionary and decisive.

There are loads of books and resources that describe each of the Types in greater depth. You will also learn more about each of the Personality Types as you read through the chapters and see how your Type comes out in managing big decisions, working with customers and coaching people, as well as choosing how to exercise, look after your children and go shopping.

# Natasha Graham

Natasha was responsible for one of my key rites of passage in the world of Personality Type—she provided my first Type feedback session when she was my mentor at the company I had just joined. I've endeavoured since then to replicate how she ran that session—as a coach she showed curiosity and enthusiasm, yet she also gave me the time and space to reach my own understanding and conclusions.

I've had the privilege to work with Natasha countless times since then, and I also can't count the number of times that she's saved my bacon, mostly from problems of my own creation. I always know that if we're working together then the work gets done, and done well. But the reason I always look forward working with her is her willingness to share her knowledge, experience and skills.

Natasha has successfully run NRG Associates for eight years, supporting a wide range of organisations, including healthcare and fitness. That's why I'm so pleased that Natasha has agreed to share some of her latest work in the area of applying Type to exercise.

Gareth

# ∷ Personality and Exercise

By Natasha Graham

## Introduction

I started ballet dancing when I was four years old and loved it from the very start. I liked the disciplined moves and clear steps and sequences that I had to learn. This appealed to my need to please and to get things right. I knew what I had to learn and I was able do the required moves to achieve the results. As a child I always liked to conform and stick to the rules, I liked to know what was expected of me so that I could achieve exactly that. Actually, when I think about it, this hasn't changed much as an adult! I liked the consistency and routine of dance while also allowing expression of my body. I began to expand my dancing classes to include National and jazz. I danced for 14 years, taking all the exams, taking part in shows, festivals and regular performances. At university I carried it on as a hobby but nothing more. After the birth of my first child I wanted to get fit again and try to get my body back, so I joined a local adult ballet class. I wanted to exercise in a way that I was used to and one which I knew I could do.

In my twenties, my fitness-mad brother persuaded me to try out a few different types of exercise. I went to kick boxing classes with him and also tried various new classes. Unfortunately, this did not last long – these activities did not come naturally to me and I felt a bit uncomfortable and out of sync. Interestingly, having spent 15 years as an MBTI® practitioner and trainer, I have now realised that these different exercise activities did not suit my Type. I much prefer the tried-and-tested, and traditional forms of exercise.

A couple of years ago I was asked to run a series of MBTI® sessions for groups of personal trainers and support staff at a large chain of gyms across the UK. The aim of this work was to enable them to understand their members better, in a bid to increase retention of membership at these gyms. During the design phase of this work, I recognised that individual preferences would have a significant impact on a person's motivation to continue attending the gym and to maintain their exercise programme. This would also be influenced by the style and approach of the gym staff and personal trainers. By understanding their own Types, the trainers were able to adjust their approach accordingly for different members, in the same way that a sales executive may use Type to tailor their sales pitch to the person in front of them.

This got me thinking more broadly about exercise and the role that personality plays within that. How does one get started? What kind of exercise do we enjoy? Where and when do we like to exercise? What motivates us? What puts us off? How can we sustain it? How can we fit it into our busy lives on a regular basis?

The existing research in this area shows that people who take up activities that play to the interests of their personality are more likely to stick with it and have greater overall fitness and enjoyment from their workouts. By understanding personality in relation to exercise, one can gain a greater sense of motivation and sustainability. This system is based upon my time working with Type in a range of settings, alongside my specific research and interviews with people about their exercise and fitness experiences.

When I analysed all the Types I found that there were four main groups. I refer to these as the Exercise Elements, and the table below shows you where each of the 16 Personality Types links to an each Element.

### Exercise Elements

| Earth | ESTJ, ESFJ, ISTJ, ISFJ |
|-------|------------------------|
| Air   | ENTP, ENFP, INTP, INFP |
| Fire  | ESTP, ESFP, ISTP, ISFP |
| Water | ENTJ, ENFJ, INTJ, INFJ |

Type experts will recognise this as the four perceiving functions, that is, introverted Sensing ($S^i$), extraverted Sensing ($S^e$), introverted iNtuition

(N$^i$) and extraverted iNtuition (Ne). For some Types this will be their dominant function, for others it will be their auxiliary function.

## Earth Types

### Overview

The Earth Types are ESTJ, ESFJ, ISTJ and ISFJ. Those of you more familiar with Type dynamics will have noticed these all have S and J in their profile, also known as introverted Sensing. Earth Types like to lead steady and organised lives. They rely on past experience to inform their decisions and actions, and will be able to recall prior experiences when needed. These Types observe the details of things that interest them and will be guided by factual information from the world around them.

### Exercise

In relation to exercise, they like to plan what activities they are going to do and when. They prefer to have an exercise routine in place and are likely to put a fair amount of detail and structure into it. Earth Types prefer the tried-and-tested forms of exercise where they are sure there are beneficial and tangible results. They are likely to be put off by fads or the latest craze.

One of the main motivators for Earth Types is commitment and consistent improvement. Once they are committed to their routine they are unlikely to give it up or put it off without very good reason. They do not appreciate unexpected complications which could get in the way of their schedule.

Earth Types like to take a step-by-step approach to their exercise routine and will be keen to see a steady improvement towards their goals. They will often measure their progress and will be keen to monitor themselves to ensure they are achieving results.

Safety and preparation are also important to Earth Types. They will prefer a predictable environment and proven exercise methods. These

Types will enjoy following a particular programme, route or schedule with established guidelines. They like familiarity and being able to push themselves further within a safe and comfortable environment. Ideally, their programmes will have been designed to maximise their personal improvement and ensure their safety.

### Felix, Marketing Executive, Swindon UK, ESTJ

I like everything to be organised and I like to plan when I am going to exercise so that I have eaten well before, I have been to the loo, etc. and it fits into my day's activities. I enjoy setting myself challenges but these are usually pretty achievable, for example, 10k/1 hour. I have never had the guts to push the boat out for something really tough like a marathon. I like to log all my activity so I can see how I have performed.

I enjoy both exercising alone and with friends but I get frustrated if I can't achieve the intensity I am after, for example, a game of tennis may not give me the same physical satisfaction as a run. If I go to, say, a spinning class and don't feel I had the intensity, I view it as wasted time as opposed to a new experience.

### Catherine, Production Manager, Manchester UK, ESFJ

I have always done some form of exercise - dancing in my teens, tae kwon do at university, going to the gym and aerobics in my early twenties. I began exercising more and running, specifically, after my Dad died – partly because he used to run when he had been younger and also because whilst I was going to the gym, etc. and doing workouts, I wasn't especially fit. I enjoyed the routine of running – I began really slowly but built up to doing 10K runs, half marathons and then a marathon.

## Marie, Nurse, Oxford UK, ISTJ

I enjoy exercise which is steady and methodical. I don't like taking unnecessary risks or just going for it. I prefer to keep track of my progress, for example, I time distance, speed, strokes in pool, etc. For me it's not about being the fastest but about getting better or within my chosen goal of speed. I like to increase my goals each year, making sure that I achieve them. My personal motivation is to get healthy and live longer, avoiding disease linked to sedentary lifestyle and to be a slim, active mother and grandmother!

I find the use of repetition helps me to concentrate, for example, counting reps/pedals on bike on big hills, 10 in saddle, and 10 out, spelling out long words with pedal or counting lengths in the pool in different ways. I don't have time to be messing around, I plan my schedule and stick to it.

*Top five exercise tips for Earth Types:*

1. Choose a form of exercise which allows for routine and schedules
2. Set incremental goals to work towards
3. Monitor your progress towards achieving your goals
4. Try out traditional, tried-and-tested forms of exercise or activity
5. Check the safety elements before starting.

*Three things to avoid:*

1. The latest fad or unproven forms of exercise
2. Messy or chaotic environments
3. Unexpected complications – make sure you are prepared and safety elements are checked.

## Air Types

### Overview

The Air fitness Types are ENTP, ENFP, INTP and INFP. They all have N and P in their profile, also known as extraverted iNtuition. Air Types tend to be people who have a lot of energy and enthusiasm and will often lead very full, busy lives. They enjoy exploring new possibilities and ideas and they scan the environment for opportunities to try something new.

### Exercise

In relation to exercise and fitness they will continue this theme, often searching for variety in the type of exercise they choose to take on. Air Types are usually optimistic people, and particularly like to focus on the future. They will tend to see exercise as an important element of future health, well-being and longevity.

One of the most important motivators around exercise for Air Types is the idea of keeping a healthy mind and body. They love the kick they get from exercising, and will particularly enjoy the rush of endorphins, the energy and the general 'feel good' factor it creates. Air Types like to stay in shape and they view their health as top priority to enable them to continue living full and rich lives. Once exercise is part of their lives they become very frustrated if their body won't allow them to continue due to illness or injury.

Exercise has to be convenient and fit in easily for the Air Types. They like an expedient approach without obstacles or unnecessary decisions getting in their way. For example, having to set up equipment before being able to exercise could put off an Air Type. They would rather be able to just get on with it, especially as their lives are usually very busy.

Air Types will often say they don't need routine or familiarity to exercise, they are happy to 'go with the flow'. For example, if working away on business, Air Types will be happy to join in with opportunities to keep them active, such as running with a client or joining a local class. It is not as important to them as it is to other Types to have familiar surroundings.

The Air Types like a good challenge and will particularly enjoy pushing themselves when it comes to exercise. They like to get the best out of their workouts and may need to be careful not to lose sight of the needs of their bodies. They can sometimes get caught up in the 'rush' and not notice the messages their body is sending.

### Rich, Entrepreneur, New York, USA, ENTP

I exercise because it gives me energy, allows me to do anything I want ... as I know and I trust that my body can do it ... it's a happiness drug, anti-ageing drug and the best energy, productive and head clearing drug there is. To me it's like a massive can of natural Red Bull and makes you feel alive! If you have watched the film Limitless – it's the closest you can get to that drug! I believe strongly that we are designed to move and we must respect that our prehistoric brain doesn't understand much else other than basic signals from our bodies so we need to tell it we are alive, that we are well, that we are supporting 'the tribe' and adding to society and to the world. It repays us with energy and positivity. Our bodies are awesome machines and it's amazing what we can do. I love variety and pushing myself physically and mentally to see what can be achieved. Most of all it's about energy for me, ensuring I feel good, productive and in general awesome!

## Cliff, Fitness fanatic and Business Owner, Seattle, USA, INTP

I love to exercise whenever and wherever I can – I like to turn exercise into something fun, for example, I pretend that I 'swim to work every morning' (by going for a swim in my gym pool downstairs!) and if I go snorkelling or diving I like to imagine I am James Bond. I love variety in everything I do including exercise and keeping fit – I will try all the different types of exercise on offer and have built my business on believing that keeping variety and new things in your workout routine is key to staying engaged.

## Louise, Designer, Buckinghamshire, UK, ENFP

I love to exercise with friends so I can be distracted by them and I also feel embarrassed if I was to give up in front of them! I mainly exercise because I fundamentally know it is healthy for my mind and body, and I don't want to be fat! I like to be busy but I make sure I have regular time to exercise and feel those endorphins flowing. If I don't exercise I start feeling a little concerned and panicky! It is that feel good factor that keeps me going ☺

*Top five exercise tips for Air Types:*

1. Allow for variety and novelty in your choice of exercise
2. Look for something with a challenge
3. Think of the future benefits
4. Find a form of exercise which is convenient for your lifestyle
5. Clear potential obstacles to your exercise – make sure any equipment is easily accessible.

*Three things to avoid:*

1. Overlooking the needs of your body
2. Getting too caught up in busy everyday life to allow time to exercise
3. Interruptions to your exercise.

## Fire Types

### Overview

The Fire Types are ESTP, ESFP, ISTP and ISFP. They all share S and P, also known as extraverted Sensing. They experience life through their five senses. They like to get involved with the physical world, and will enjoy sensory experiences. Extraverted Sensors can be risk-takers as they enjoy the adrenaline rush that accompanies these types of activities. They may even invent or create elements within their everyday life to give them that adrenaline rush or feeling of being alive. They are usually good at improvising and responding in the moment especially in crisis situations or at times when a quick response or reaction is needed.

### Exercise

In relation to exercise, Fire Types particularly enjoy the physical world and are often drawn to activities which take them outside within the natural environment. They are very attuned to and observant of the world around them. They like exercise to blend into everyday life, rather than specifically scheduling in activities in a routine manner. For example, they may choose to walk, cycle or run to work rather than take transport – where transport is essential they will find ways to incorporate exercise around it such as cycling to the train station and running to the office at the other end. Some Fire Types will even go as far as to incorporate exercise into their essential daily activities, for example, doing lunges while waiting for the toast to pop up.

One of the most important motivators for Fire Types is stimulation. They like to feel alive, to live in the moment, to experience their bodies. As such, these are the Types most likely to enjoy training for an event or competition as it gives them a focus and they love the challenge of a good contest. Purpose is also important – they do not like to exercise just for exercise sake. Fire Types tend to be quick-thinking and especially enjoy a challenge. They are usually more than happy to 'jump in' and exercise spontaneously rather than planning in advance or setting out clear structures and routines.

They are unlikely to be put off by the weather. Being resourceful people, Fire Types will simply adapt appropriately to the weather conditions. They are much more likely to be put off by repetitive, indoor exercise where they feel confined and restricted. For example, swimming lengths in an indoor pool is boring to these Types, but jumping into an open lake and seeing if they can make it to the other side is far more appealing, even if the water is cold!

### Clara, Fitness Manager, New York USA, ESTP

I love moving my body in just about every single way, shape and form – whether it's a high intensity class, yoga or hiking up the biggest mountain on the most difficult path we can find with my other half. I'm more than a little competitive, and am drawn to ways of working out that enable me to monitor and track my performance against both myself and others and will constantly push myself to my limit. Often I'll find myself moving just for the fun of it and would even go so far as to say I'm a little fascinated by how amazing my body is at being able to do all of the things I ask it to do – for example, I'll suddenly end up doing some squats or high knees whilst brushing my teeth, or I'll see how many times I can run up and down stairs in the time it takes the kettle to boil (2.5 for 2 cups!). My recent obsession is my FitBit activity tracker... I love 'competing' with myself and friends each day on how many steps we're doing, and it really makes the difference on taking a bedtime walk or doing some last-minute star jumps to make sure I hit my goal!

## George, Investment Banker, London UK, ISTP

I love training in the great outdoors. Running in the woods and getting lost knowing I will find my way back, finishing covered in mud. Open water swimming as opposed to the pool, to the point where I avoid the swimming pool but would jump at the chance of going to a lake or river with my wetsuit. Cycling up a steep hill because it is there. I much prefer runs and triathlons that are off-road and are the "hardest" you can do. I can't bear the attitude that it's ok just to take part and finish, if you're in it you go hard, start to finish (I might say I'll be happy just to finish an extreme event but really I want to smash it, I will train harder because of this). I fit in training when I can but mainly that's because of my working hours. I can't get up early to go for a run because I already get up very early to go to work. So I run to the office or cycle to a station further down the line. I will add on to my 'training commute' if I feel like. Cycling longer because the weather is nice or running down a different path to see where it goes.

## Hannah, General Manager, Bath UK, ESFP

One of the best things about keeping active for me is having no fear of any kind of physical activity and complete confidence in myself and my body – whether its joining a friend to try out a new class, signing up for an adventure race, carrying the heavy boxes when helping a friend move or eliciting shouts of 'coooool' from my favourite little people when I can climb the big tree! I consider being physically active a defining part of my character and am sure all of my friends and family would agree.

*Top five exercise tips for Fire Types:*

1. Try exercise that takes you outdoors.
2. Make sure it fits into your everyday life.
3. Choose an exercise that will push you and help you feel alive.
4. Have a go at competitive exercising (with yourself or others).
5. Look for something practical and action-focused.

*Three things to avoid:*

1. Static and routine types of exercise.
2. Repetitious exercise.
3. Exercise without a purpose.

## Water Types

### Overview

The Water Types are INTJ, INFJ, ENTJ and ENFJ. They all have N and J in their profile, also known as introverted iNtuition. They have a rich inner world of connections, patterns, meanings and concepts. They report having lots of ideas and connections constantly bubbling around in their mind, with intricate links and long range visions of the future.

### Exercise

In relation to exercise, Water Types enjoy the mental escape they can get from exercising. They like to connect their mind and body and will report a sense of freedom in being able to lose themselves in the exercise. A positive, and ideally familiar environment, is important to Water Types to allow them this opportunity to 'zone out', whether that be to reflect on their thoughts and ideas, or to completely switch off their very active minds for a short period. They may become distracted or irritated by too much interaction unless, of course, the real purpose of their exercise activity is to be sociable! Water Types like to devise their own exercise programmes based on their research. They will make sure they are well-informed in the area they chose to pursue, this way they can feel alignment with their inner vision. They don't like 'fads and quick fixes', it needs to be something which fits for them and can give them long-term benefit. Water Types like to have a clear sense of purpose and usually a goal around why they are exercising. They will enjoy achieving the results they have set for themselves.

One of the most important motivators for this Water Types is their inner vision, and the ability to match this to reality. They like to really understand the activities they choose to partake in, and the potential future benefits of it. These Types will report spending time researching and learning about their chosen area of exercise.

They will typically create structure and take an organised approach to their exercise, although this may not be visible to the outer world. They will know for themselves that what they have created and devised is well researched and well planned. A positive environment is particularly important to Water Types. Most say they would not continue if the environment around them was not conducive to or did not fit in with their vision and expectations.

## Angela, Psychologist, Oxford, UK, INTJ

The only thing that floats my boat is yoga, which I could do all day. I like it because it has an actual context and is not just about exercise. It has a philosophy behind it, is, and it is based on your own experience of the postures rather than having someone shouting at you to do better. Additionally, I see it having a long term benefit – I hope to be able to put my own socks on until I die! I like that it is individual and always cringe when we have to work in pairs, but I find it hard to motivate myself to do it alone so I have to go to a class. Definitely not for the social experience though.

Being me, of course I had to nerd it up, so I did the British Wheel foundation course a few years ago to learn more about the philosophy and the other 'limbs of yoga'. I used to think the chanting bit was just showing off, but now I understand that it has a purpose (vibrations resonate at different chakra points in the body) I am happy to chant away.

## Bert, Executive Coach, London, UK, INTJ

I enjoy exercising for the mental and physical 'feel good' factor that I experience afterwards and the frustrating 'not feeling good' if I don't. There is also the rational justification that I know that it's good for me, both physically and mentally. I have set routines and jogging routes but if I'm away in a strange place then I'm equally happy to go to a gym and run on the treadmill, mainly because getting lost and having the routine broken is bad news. It's much more an internal thing then interacting with the environment, it's more about an inner game and inner place that I go to. I could have killed the guy who tried to start up a conversation with me from a neighbouring treadmill!

**Miranda, Community Arts Charity Leader, Maidenhead UK, INFJ**

I love dancing, it allows me to switch my brain off and experience the rhythm. I also enjoy yoga and pilates because it is exercise with an ethos and spirituality and it frees the mind from thinking rubbish but connects mind to body. I'm not into the latest exercise fad, I'd rather do what's right for me. A positive environment is essential to me otherwise I will not go!

*Top five exercise tips for Water Types:*

1. Align your choice of exercise to your personal vision
2. Make sure it has a purpose
3. Create your own exercise programme
4. Research and understand it to help keep you motivated
5. Integrate it into your lifestyle.

*Three things to avoid:*

1. Too much direction from others
2. Uncomfortable or unpleasant environments
3. Interruptions to your exercise

### Exercise Elements in Action

This approach to Type is already being utilised by some exercise coaches and businesses. I would hope that other professionals in the fitness industry will see the value of the Exercise Elements approach in helping their clients and customers to develop more suitable and sustainable exercise programmes. What works for one client will not be the same as what works for another. Therefore, having an understanding of the Personality Types of each individual client will help more people to reach their exercise goals.

In addition, I would envisage that the Exercise Elements approach will also be valuable and easily utilised for those of us simply wanting to find exercise that we can sustain over time. This outlines that it is not just willpower at work here – our Personality Type will have an impact on what exercise we choose and what will keep us going.

It has been a very interesting and motivating journey to research this area. I have particularly enjoyed hearing about other people's exercising habits and motivations. Initially, people tended to assume that everyone is motivated to exercise in a similar way or that certain activities or patterns would help to get others started. By interviewing individuals, couples and groups I was able to hear the interactions and responses to these findings as well. For example, one husband realised that the reason he had never managed to get his wife to join him in his exercising was because they are very different Types, and he was actually putting her off by trying to persuade her to try out the latest craze! It has also confirmed to me that my choices for keeping fit are valid and don't need to be changed – they suit who I am and they work for me.

# Linn Brynildsen

Linn worked for many years as a business psychologist, which is where I first worked with her. It was no surprise to me that, with her vision and empathy, she became an expert in leadership development and emotional intelligence.

I have witnessed many times her ability to help her clients to apply the principles of psychology to their lives. This meant that is was also no surprise to me that in more recent years she has successfully created the mayamin.co.uk website, which provides practical, down-to-earth advice for parents on the latest psychological research into parenting and child development.

It is her research and experience in the psychology of parenting that has led to this chapter where Linn will discuss her approach to looking at the different Psychological Parenting Types and how those relate to different Types of children.

I have worked with Linn on many projects and I was delighted when she agreed to work with me on an exciting new project – raising two children of our own!

Gareth

# :: Type Parenting–Stop. Look. Breathe.

By Linn Brynildsen

## Introduction

It's a few years ago now that the realisation came to me for the first time. I was in the bathroom in the middle of the night and I looked in the mirror. I looked so tired, yet I was wide awake. I felt like it had been months since I had actually *seen* myself when I was looking into the mirror. All those other times I must have been looking *through* the mirror, like when you stare into the distance simply because that's the only thing your tired brain is allowing you to do. Yes, I realised, I'm a mum. Since that night I've had many more moments of true realisation that I'm a parent, and most of those moments are ones of sheer, utter, mad happiness. And pride. No-one and nothing in the world makes you as happy or as proud as your children. Even when you're so tired you could fall asleep standing up.

Most days as a parent are wonderful, exciting and awesome. Some days, though, we wonder if we can get away with putting our children to bed a few hours earlier than usual. Just to get a few moments of peace. Parenting can be exhausting, and yet we put pressure on ourselves to be the 'perfect' parent. "I must get this baby to sleep!", "How do I get this child to stop drawing on the walls!", "I feel I'm the only one with the child screaming at me in the supermarket", "I wish my little one could learn to share and not growl at other children". We also expend a lot of energy to remain cool, calm and collected even in the face of the most inspired tantrums. If you think about it, perfect parenting is an impossible mission. But more 'peaceful' parenting is definitely achievable.

### The Magic of Awareness

Each child is unique. The same parenting methods rarely work on two different children, and sometimes not even on the one child you

19

thought you had sussed out! So we search through the huge amount of information, advice and models out there. There are lots of great tips to be found, but personally, I've found it somewhat exhausting, mostly because the solution never fits quite like a glove. We have two children, and they are so different in what helps them sleep, what makes them listen to us, what frustrates them, and what 'tickles' them the most. Children's unique nature is the real challenge, but it's also a parent's secret weapon! To understand our children's Personality Type is to find the solution we are seeking. Through their likes, dislikes, actions and reactions, they are in fact telling us how to best parent them. They are telling us what works and what doesn't. Our own Personality Type naturally influences our parenting style, but it's when you allow your child's Personality Type to influence your parenting that 'real magic' happens.

So, instead of parenting our way, doing it *their* way will open roads to a world of parenting where you feel less frustrated and more successful as you are in tune with your little one. From my own experience, I can also tell you that your child will feel less frustrated and more successful too! For example, my daughter needs harmony and many of her actions come from a desire to create or keep harmony. My son wants to do everything himself and really wants us to trust him to find things out in his own way and his own time. When I get it right, I see how cooperative they really are and also how confidently they do things because they feel supported in doing it their own way.

A great coach once shared a very useful tool with me, which I love applying to parenting – *Stop. Look. Breathe. Stop* talking, stop doing, and put frustration aside. *Look* at your child's behaviour and reactions and try to understand where they're coming from. *Breathe* – a good tip in its own right, as it allows you to calm. You can then really listen to what your child is telling you: what's actually driving their behavior? Stop, look, breathe – these three simple words help to increase your awareness, allowing you to better see your child's unique characteristics and how best to parent them.

## Your Parenting Style

I've used Personality Type for years both in and out of work, and seen the power it has to increase people's awareness, their confidence and effectiveness. Our Personality Type also tells us a great deal about how we are likely to be as parents, what we emphasise, value and encourage in bringing up a child. Understanding your own parenting style helps explain why parenting sometimes comes easily, and other times leaves you feeling bewildered. I've found that certain aspects of Personality Type are particularly useful in this area, and to make things simple here I'll be talking about four different parenting styles:

1. The Playmate (who all have S and P in their Type)
2. The Protector (who all have S and J in their Type)
3. The Soul Guide (who all have N and F in their Type)
4. The Mentor (who all have N and T in their Type)

These are inspired by the in-depth research by David Keirsey.

### The Playmate
Personality Types ESTP, ESFP, ISTP, ISFP

What delights me about the Playmate Type is how they love listening to the child within and going with their impulses. They engage in play and adventures with a natural ease and thorough enjoyment. Their natural way is a 'live-and-let-live' approach, giving their children plenty of freedom to explore opportunities and to learn by getting stuck into things. Because Playmate parents enjoy living in the moment and seizing every exciting opportunity, they want the same joys for their children. They give them a 'long leash' to allow them to go where their curiosity and adventure takes them. And, of course, they are probably the ones running right behind their children to take part in the fun.

Lots of parenting advice talks about the importance of routine, but for Playmate parents routine does not come naturally. They enjoy going with the flow rather than planning ahead. Discipline is not something they want to think about too much, probably because they personally don't want to be guided or "restricted" by rules and regulations. Sometimes directions are needed, of course, and some Playmate parents then expect their children to follow their decisions or instructions without fuss, while others may find more fun and subtle ways to get their little ones to do what they ask. But of all the Parenting Types they are least likely to want to supervise.

Playmate parents encourage children's adventurous side and see mistakes as a natural consequence of exploring; as they say, "you learn by falling down". For some children, being given such free rein is perfect, and they thrive on being able to explore at will. Playmate parents may find it challenging if their children are cautious and much less adventurous than they are themselves. Some children need more rules and want more supervision to feel safe or able to explore. Many children also thrive on routine, as predictability and familiarity provide them with feelings of security.

*The Playmate Parenting Type at their best:*

- Loves trying exciting new things with their children.
- Is always up for playing outside and doing active things.
- Enjoys exploring and discovering – seeing life as an adventure.
- Indulges in doing things in the moment – setting everything else aside to enjoy the here and now with their children.
- Role models for going with the flow and seeing challenges as exciting.

*Challenges for the Playmate Parenting Type:*

- Conforming when this is needed, such as at school or various group gatherings. "Why not bend the rules if that makes it more fun or interesting?"
- Seeing that giving too much freedom and too few constraints could lead to injury.
- Providing rules and giving consistent, clear guidance.
- Noticing that some children focus more on thoughts and feelings, and stopping to engage in deeper conversations.
- Seeing that some children wish to understand how things work, and engage more in ideas, thoughts and fantasy than doing something for the thrill of the moment.

## Chris – a Playmate parent in action

I'm the one who 'takes over' when it comes to doing sports, going camping or finding new fun ways to play. I guess I enjoy it just as much as the kids do. I remember last winter when it was really icy outside, my two daughters held onto the car, sliding along behind me on their boots. I drove very slowly down the drive, but it gave them a thrill.

If we do too much routine or we're in one place for too long, I need to go and do something. I don't mind so much if the bedtime routine is slipping, but when enough is enough I expect them to listen straight away. I don't think I pay too much attention to whether homework has been done, someone else can look after that!

27% of people are likely to have the Playmate parenting style (from a representative sample of 1634 people from the UK population. Source: MBTI Step 1 Manual. European Data Supplement. OPP. 2011.)

## *The Protector*
Personality Types ESTJ, ESFJ, ISTJ, ISFJ

What I admire about Protector parents is the importance they place on family and traditions, and the ease with which they remain grounded and consistent in their approach. They like structure and are keen to introduce and follow a good routine with their little ones. Protector parents provide clear guidance and instructions for their children, helping them find a good way to do things. They feel happier and more relaxed when they can plan ahead, making sure there is time for both work and play, and that the two don't interfere. They take a 'safer' approach than the Playmate, feeling they can parent best when they are in control of what their little ones are doing and where they are going. They love family trips and spending time enjoying nature, preferring it when everyone is gathered together and they are able to look after each other. Some Protector Types live to care for their children, others say the most important thing for them is to show their children the 'right way'. But what all parents with the Protector Parenting Type have in common is their focus on family values, loyalty and fitting in with how things work best.

Protector parents are dutiful and will teach their children about the values of being helpful and trustworthy. Learning to look after and support one another will be at the heart of how they bring up their children. They don't favour 'going against the stream', and they want to make sure children are helpful and dutiful at school or any other social gathering. The Protector Parenting Type enjoys maintaining traditions and gathering people around them, family in particular. As they would say, "This is how we've always done it", so it feels comfortable and satisfying. They will also have vivid memories and detailed stories of previous fun and gatherings.

Doing the right thing is important to Protector parents, as well as safeguarding their little ones. They create an environment where routines, rules and discipline will be applied clearly and consistently. They may find it difficult if their children keep pushing for independence or roam free without taking enough notice of safety, rules or the impact of their actions.

*The Protector Parenting Type at their Best:*

- Plans family outings and seeing the sights.
- Loves nature and playing outside.
- Introduces and follows routines that make sure things run smoothly, and applies a consistent approach.
- Sees things as they are and tells detailed, entertaining stories of things that have happened.
- Role models for trustworthiness and loyalty.

*Challenges for the Protector Parenting Type:*

- Going with the flow and the unexpected, loosening the reins with children who desire the freedom to explore.
- Taking risks and embracing change.
- Encouraging children to step out of their comfort zone and rely on their own instincts to choose the right way forward.
- Noticing that as well as being helpful, some children need to hear how they are standing out from the crowd, their special contribution.
- Accepting that some children want to find their own way, not conform to what is 'expected' of them.

## Natalie – a Protector Parent's story

Weekends are for family time and outings, and I dislike it when someone upsets this structure. Now that my children are more into their sports and activities at the weekends, I make sure we all go together when we can.

I love that my children are active, but I almost feel sick when I see them climb up very high or balance on the highest point in the park.

I love the playground and making things with my children, and I see things for what they are. I remember putting on a rubber glove to clean something in the kitchen, and as I looked at my son I tried to think of something funny. Now, what could the glove be? All I could think was, "it's a rubber glove". I don't know how people come up with fantastical things where a glove can become a dragon, a monster, or even an animal or a plane.

About 50% of people are likely to have the Protector parenting style.

## The Soul Guide
Personality Types ENFJ, ENFP, INFJ, INFP

What I value about this Parenting Type is the desire to be as nurturing and supportive as possible, to form a strong, close relationship with their children. The Soul Guide parent seeks to really understand each child's individual needs and thoughts, and love spending time with their little ones to find out what they enjoy. The Soul Guide parent creates a home environment where harmony rules and they want their children to be considerate and accepting of others. Children should be able to express what's important to them, and the Soul Guide parent will use this knowledge to help each child grow into who they are supposed to be. They personally have a strong need to be true to themselves, and wish for their children to find their authentic selves and be happy.

The Soul Guide parent communicates important values and they talk to their children from when they are very young about the ways of the world, about ideals, thoughts and dreams. It's important to them that their children feel positive about themselves, and they make sure that each child knows how special they are. When their children are upset, the Soul Guide parent will always want to be there to help them through it, give cuddles and listen to their thoughts and feelings. It can be very upsetting for this Parenting Type if they feel unable to comfort their children, or if they feel they are not allowed – "Why won't they let me in?"

The Soul Guide's need for harmony often makes for a calm environment, but with other Types around them this can also create stress for this Parent Type. They find it difficult when there is disagreement, and particularly when others don't seem to mind or they don't make the effort to work things out and restore harmony. It can also be challenging for them if their children are too independent or *too* busy exploring to engage in real conversation with them.

*The Soul Guide Parent at their Best:*

- Loves spending time with their children and value them for who they are.
- Revels in creating an environment of harmony and good relationships.
- Engages in meaningful conversations where children feel heard and understood.
- Enjoys fantastical games and stories, using imagination in play and finding amusements in situations.
- Role model for empathy and authenticity.

*Challenges for the Soul Guide Parent:*

- Understanding that some children just want excitement and to live for the moment rather than engaging in a deep, sharing relationship.
- Providing specific, practical guidance for children who wish to know exactly what is expected of them.
- Stepping out of dreams, thoughts and ideas to allow for more realism and objective, rational views.
- Noticing the here and now, truly enjoying the moment without thinking about the future.
- Realising it's not a personal failing, but an achievement, when children want to be independent and no longer need that helping hand.

## Annie – a Soul Guide's vision

I love listening to my children talking about school, friendships, thoughts and dreams. I piece it all together to understand what they're all about and how they are unique. It's wonderful to see the little personalities coming through and watch their development. Reading time is so much fun, especially getting excited about adventure stories and listening to what the kids think might happen next.

It's important that everyone gets along, and that we can talk things through to settle disagreements. I admit I feel stressed when there are arguments, and if I'm the one causing the disharmony that's even worse. But most of the time, I manage to restore peace and make sure everyone is ok.

14% of people are likely to have the Soul Guide parenting style (about 10% of men, 17.5% of women).

### *The Mentor*
Personality Types INTJ, INTP, ENTP, ENTJ

What I marvel at about the Mentor Types is how well they encourage their children to be independent and to think for themselves. They enjoy seeing their little ones strive to master things on their own, yet provide guidance eloquently when needed. They love discussing all kinds of things and encourage their children's curiosity to find out about how the world works. The Mentor Parenting Type will be interested in being the 'best' parent, following their desire to be competent in everything they do. Even before the baby is born they will find themselves reading up on the latest ideas and advice – so long as it's well researched!

Mentor parents will usually take the time to explain rules and discipline methods to their children, after all they wouldn't personally follow rules that didn't seem logical! They want their children to understand why they are being asked to do something, and not just follow rules for the sake of it. It's also important to them that their children don't 'blindly' follow in other people's footsteps, but instead consider and question, or even better find their own way. Mentor Parenting Types can find it challenging when children are acting or reacting irrationally or when emotions are running high. "Why won't they calm down so I can help them?" It's frustrating for them when children won't listen to reason.

Mentor parents may not follow others' rules or routines, but they do like efficiency, and therefore encourage their family to follow routines they can see help make things run more smoothly.

*The Mentor Parenting Type at their Best:*

- Encourages their children to think for themselves and find the answers.
- Loves jigsaws, board games and fantasy books.
- Gives children freedom to do things their own way, not worrying about how others do it.
- Enjoys finding things out together with their children, and letting them help with 'grown-up' tasks, such as changing batteries in a toy, fixing the door on the shed or making 'Gruffalo piles' out of autumn leaves.
- Mentors independence and finding the best ways forward.

*Challenges for the Mentor Parenting Types:*

- Providing children who need it with clear rules and guidance on how to do things.
- Understanding that not all children will thrive on independence or feel excited about finding their own way.
- Making sure there is room for understanding each individual child and expressing emotions.
- Seeing that there is a place for community and traditions, and communicating this to their children.
- Remembering that all children will get irrational and carried away with their emotions at times.

## Jonathan – a Mentor Parent enjoying the path

I enjoy watching my children find their own way and realise they are capable of so much. If they really get stuck, I will of course help them, and I enjoy sharing with them what I know or finding answers together with them. I'm not particularly interested in what everyone else does, I want my child to do their own thing, follow their interest and do that well.

I'd say I get very excited when the kids show a keen interest in how and why something works. We have fun planting seeds in the garden and follow the growing process of plants and flowers, talking about the interplay between everything in nature. I also love building with them – Lego constructions, jigsaw puzzles, marble tumble, you name it.

About 10% of people are likely to have the Mentor parenting style (18% of men, 7% of women).

## Your child's way

A child's personality shines through from the start. Although children will try out different styles through their childhood, most research says that personality 'sets' between the ages 3-5 years. Of course, we keep developing and learning throughout life, but our Personality Type – our preferred, most 'natural' ways of being in the world and doing things – remains constant. It's our 'base camp', which we build on and develop from.

As with the Parenting Types, I will use four different Types of children to give you a powerful and easy-to-use guide when it comes to adapting your parenting style. Yes, each child will express their Personality Type in their own unique way. However, children of the same Type do share a great deal – they, enjoy similar games, view the world in the same way and respond best to certain ways of parenting. Using these Types helps us to look for options and to learn from what's worked for other parents. Herein lies the power of Personality Type for parenting.

The four Types of children are:

- Little Adventurers (SP)
- Little Helpers (SJ)
- Little Dreamers (NF)
- Little Learners (NT)

Those familiar with Type will again recognise that I've taken inspiration from David Keirsey's research into temperament.

## Little Adventurers (SP)

Children who seem to have an insatiable desire to seek out excitement and new experiences I've chosen to call Little Adventurers. While impulsivity and spontaneity are the prerogative of any child, none will revel in it more than the Little Adventurer. Parents will notice that their Little Adventurers are happiest when they have the freedom to move from one activity to the next, and when they get to do something they have never done before. Every moment is an opportunity to play, and these children will make the most of it. They may not always feel fearless, but will certainly seem fearless to others as they engage in challenges! They love being the first one to jump in the cold sea, leap from the highest point, and do the most cartwheels without stopping. If they have an audience, it's even more fun. Like any other child, they may feel a little worried at times, but their curiosity and excitement will tend to overcome their concerns.

Little Adventurers are fun and easy to get long with, and other children enjoy their company. They seem so carefree, as they have few concerns other than to truly live in the moment and notice every experience – every taste, smell, sight and sound. Their ideas of the ultimate joy would be running through high grass or muddy fields, engaging in the colours of painting or learning to play instruments. Little Adventurers love to use their bodies and delight in being outside, where they can unfold without restriction. Their curiosity tells them the grass may really be greener on the other side of the fence, so they had better jump over and take a look! Their adventures can take them high and low to places others hadn't thought of going.

It's no surprise, then, that Little Adventurers dislike having to follow rules or regulations, as this feels confining. All children get bored or restless, and all children are tempted to run with their impulses rather than follow instructions. But boredom and sitting still will be particularly hard for Little Adventurers. In such situations they will find something to fiddle with, or you may see them drift across the room, often chatting to themselves or others.

My main advice with the Little Adventurer Type is to find what they enjoy doing and use this to capture their attention. Adults may think it's almost impossible for these children to focus on a task, but once they are interested they will enjoy really getting into it and stay with it for a long time.

*Parent Traps:*

- Telling the Little Adventurer to *stop* doing something, and trying to *make* them stop by restricting their freedom or talking about negative long term consequences. Why? Because they just think of the moment, "of course I want treats tomorrow, but that's tomorrow. Right now I really want to find out what happens when I ride my bike down the sofa".
- Trying to direct them, to get them to follow routines and regulations. This will just want to make them go in the opposite direction. In fact, parents find that Little Adventurers are more persistent than other children when it comes to resisting and testing limit. For example, going against the rules and sticking a pea up their nose when told not to (even after having had other small objects removed before, at the doctor's office).

*Parent Tips:*

- Find ways to encourage the little Adventurer to *start* showing you more desirable behaviour. They want things to happen, so appeal to their love of 'doing' and make what you need from them sound fun. Make sure you praise and reward them 'in the moment' when they are acting in positive ways. Rewarding positive behaviour and ignoring the negative is a golden key when it comes to discipline tactics for little Adventurers.
- Remember that they find challenges hard to resist and that they like seeing the pay-off of their actions. If trying out a new behaviour feels like an exciting competition rather than an instruction, the little Adventurer will feel compelled to take part. "I want to be the fastest at getting dressed so I get to choose our snack for the day."
- To help them focus, include things they love to entice them – doing something active or engaging in something creative (music, painting, drawing). Support them in their love of action, movement and art.

## Adventurer Alice

"Alice always finds ways to bend the rules or go against decisions. We've had to become quite crafty with how we encourage her to do things. She is at her best when she can move between different activities, and she's always been agile. She'd rather cartwheel across a room than walk, and she definitely loves an audience - showing off her skills in skiing, diving and sailing. Her enthusiasm gets her sister and friends into things too."

## Adventurer Tommy

"From the moment Tommy could roll over and crawl, he'd be off the changing mat in a split second and climbing on to the windowsill! As he got older he would build a 'ladder' out of chairs and climb up to get to the cookie jar on top of the cupboards. He has lots of friends and takes most things in his stride. The school environment can feel restricting for him – he really needs a teacher who knows how to engage him."

## *Little Helpers (SJ)*

Little Helpers are the children who feel at their best in a structured environment. They want to know what is expected of them and how to play, doing what's 'right' or most helpful. Most children feel a sense of security with consistency and predictability in their surroundings, but Little Helpers are the ones who really thrive on routine and clear guidelines. They are generally more cautious than Little Adventurers, preferring to look before they leap, and love the safety of a familiar environment. They love practical games and activities where they can use instructions, organize, or make something. The instructions for their new Lego set will be followed with care and enthusiasm, and any craft or drawing activity will have precision and colour. They enjoy cooking, baking, building a den under the stairs, and setting the rules in a game – "how many do we need in each team", "how many goals before we change goalie". They also enjoy games where they are looking after people or toys, and prefer to keep their things nice and tidy. Parents will notice that their Little Helpers love it when they praise them for being organised and looking after things.

I've called them Little Helpers as this is their most desired role from a very young age, and it is how others usually see them. They love being able to help friends, siblings and adults in a practical way. With friends, they may help them tidy up or run to get things they need. They also enjoy showing others how to do something, helping them get it right.

At home, they will want to help wash the car, set the table, do dishes, or perhaps help with younger siblings. They have a strong need to feel they belong and that they are important. Little Helpers are born members. They place great importance on their family and as they grow they enjoy being part of various groups and clubs. Many children will enjoy helping with adult tasks, as they like doing what they've seen you do. But Little Helpers really relish learning from parents and other adults (or older siblings) and take pride in being responsible.

Feedback and approval is important to Little Helpers. They rely on parents and other adults to tell them that they have done a good job, and what specifically they did well – "you were feeding your little sister so nicely there", "that's such great tidying away, you put everything back in its place", "wow, that game was so much fun as you kept track and made sure we all knew what we were doing". They often thrive in a school environment, where being dutiful, helpful and working hard is rewarded. Listening to instructions and 'locking on to learning' without being distracted will be easy feats for Little Helpers. They love being given specific responsibilities, such as 'helper of the day', 'soap monitor' or looking after someone younger.

As Little Helpers rely on routine and knowing 'how things are done around here', they find big or constant change difficult. Change often means lack of clarity and direction, and it's harder to understand expectations or roles. Little Helpers will be much happier exploring or taking on new things if they know what is expected of them.

*Parent Traps:*

- Asking Little Helpers to find their own way of doing things. Rather than feeling encouraged and excited, they can feel uncomfortable and rudderless without direction or knowing the rules.
- Expecting them to embrace change or to 'get on with it' in a new environment. Little Helpers want to seek answers, knowing who is in charge, and "how do I fit in?"

*Parent Tips:*

- Little Helpers prefer an environment where everyone is in agreement on the best ways to do things. That way, they know what to do and how to be most helpful and efficient.
- If big changes are afoot, make sure the Little Helpers feel able to find something stable to hold on to, and at the very least that they know who to ask when they need direction or answers.
- Little Helpers respond well to parenting that is consistent and firm, and when parents use the same rules. They like knowing and following rules, feel safe knowing who is in charge, and feel happy that they know how to achieve praise.

## Helper Ollie

"Ollie has always been dutiful, at home and at school. He makes sure his homework is done properly, and needs to know we have prepared everything for activities going on at school. His toys all have their own place, and his football gear is always organised and ready for use. Ollie is a loyal friend and quickly settles in to a team."

## Helper Isla

"From a very young age Isla has loved a good routine and knowing what to expect. She is most definitely a 'people pleaser', and her little face beams with pride when we praise her for being helpful. We call her our little 'copy-and-paste' girl, as she always notices what we do and does the same. As a toddler she made picnics for her teddies and dolls, and now she makes breakfast for us!"

## *Little Dreamers (NF)*

Little Dreamers is the name I've given to children who, from a young age, seem to be on a quest to find their 'unique self'. They are very aware of both positive and negative feelings, often experiencing emotions more intensely than other children. They share with you (sometimes in an endless stream) their feelings, their dreams, and all the things they wonder about. Why are things the way they are? How have they come to be? Why are we here and what is coming next? They are enthusiastic, warm, and want to be noticed for bringing something special. Parents will notice that their Little Dreamers have a very natural way with others. They are genuinely interested in what is going on for those around them, and they're seen as open hearted, kind and friendly. They are guided by their intuition, and sometimes say "I just know" but may not be able to explain why or how.

Harmony is very important to Little Dreamers. They thrive in an environment that is loving and supportive and where relationships are strong. If there is conflict, they will feel insecure and will want to withdraw unless harmony is restored quickly. They are often the 'harmoniser', working to help everyone get along. For parents, it works best to explain things calmly to their Little Dreamers, and remember to show understanding for their questions and needs. Little Dreamers feel hurt and upset if they are spoken harshly to, in particular if there is no explanation afterwards. They need lots of reassurance, and being told how important they are.

Little Dreamers often enjoy school. They like learning about lots of different things, and developing relationships with children and teachers. It's important to them that they are seen as supportive and 'special', and may worry that others don't understand them or see them as significant. Little Dreamers are cooperative in play, preferring this to competitive activities. "I like it when everyone is happy and enjoying the same things". They really enjoy pretend games and create great stories with many dramatic events and colourful characters.

Little Dreamers love it when their parents read stories with them. They get really involved in the characters' feelings and experiences, and talking about what might happen next. They will ask for their favourite stories over and over, often those involving princesses and princes, wizards and fairies or other fantastical heroes and heroines. Their imagination really gets going and can lead to nightmares, so choose bedtime stories with a happy ending! Little Dreamers often become very attached to their favourite soft toy, animal or doll. It will be like a family member and best friend, part of everything they do, with 'real' feelings of its own. So whatever you do, don't lose it! (Or have a few spare ones hidden away.)

*Parent Traps:*

- Behaving impatiently with Little Dreamers, telling them to stop talking and hurry up. Although they need prompting sometimes, being able to share their thoughts and feelings is important to them.
- Thinking they will just move on if they have withdrawn from a conflicted situation. Little Dreamers feel scared and insecure if things are left unresolved, they need to know that an argument has been, or will be sorted out.

*Parent Tips:*

- Take time to listen to Little Dreamers. When time really is of the essence, interrupt them gently and explain that you can talk more later. Perhaps suggest they can 'put it behind their ear' in the meantime.
- They love that you understand them, so remember to tell your Little Dreamer every so often how they are unique and important.
- Talk about situations that have been difficult, either at home or at school. This will allow your Little Dreamers to share their experience, and also work out how to deal with it.

## Dreamer Marianne

"Marianne has always been incredibly alert to the atmosphere around her. She developed her language skills early, and is very articulate about her own emotions. She's great at making those around her feel good. She also really feels others' upset or unhappiness, and tries to make them feel better. When we play games, Marianne prefers to play cooperatively because she doesn't like it that someone has to lose."

## Dreamer Robbie

Robbie finds any disagreement between his parents very upsetting, and will try to restore harmony by saying things like "are you forgetting you're married and love each other?" He usually reflects about his day and how he got on with his class mates and teachers. He also thinks about why things are the way they are – "why are we here?", "why do we have to die", "why don't most animals live as long as us?"(and he used to get upset for the animals).

### *Little Learners*

Little Learners are the children who seem to be born with a thirst for knowledge and a desire to strive for excellence. They love learning something new, and will have more questions than any other children – "why can we sometimes see the sun and the moon at the same time?" They like being independent and finding their own way. Although all children are curious and enjoy pushing buttons, flipping light switches etc., Little Learners are the ones you find still sitting there, working it through until they have completely figured out how something works. They take things apart to understand how they function, and if you're lucky they will put them back together! Sometimes of course they may just leave the pieces in a pile, feeling satisfied that they've worked it out. Parents will notice their love of the 'what if?' process, finding out what happens if you unscrew the door handles, paint the greenhouse blue or push all the buttons inside the car at the same time.

Loving learning and being clever, Little Learners are competitive and will revel in toys or games that involve a challenge. They will think things through and form strategies to find the best way to win. Board games and computer games are usually among their top favourites. Parents will also see an inventive side as their Little Learners take over floor space with great constructions using train tracks, Lego or any suitable building blocks. They often love collecting things too, for example, stamps, toy soldiers, flowers, stones or paper aeroplanes. They get very involved in finding out about their collections and will learn how to best take care of them.

Parents will see Little Learners' strong independent streak coming through from the start. They will be more self-contained as babies and continue to be tranquil and composed. When they start playing more, it's important to them that they independently master new skills ("Tim do it himself!"). If they do get stuck, they ask for help but will only go to those who seem to be best at it ("Mamma is better at fixing things than Pappa!" or "Grandpa knows more about plants than Grandma"). Little Learners dislike others telling them what to do, think or feel. Even from a very young age, they want to decide for themselves, and will go against parents trying to direct them. Parents will find that their success depends on giving a good logical explanation for what they want their Little Learners to do. They won't easily go along with something just because you said so or because "that's how we do things". It has to make sense. It takes a bit longer, therefore, to get Little Learners into a routine or to understand social rules around things like table manners – "Why do we have to use a knife and fork? "..."Who says? "..."Well who told them?"..."But *why?*"

Little Learners love story time, in particular intrigued by science, science fiction, magic, and tales about the great feats of heroes. Like Little Dreamers, their imagination really gets going with stories they enjoy, which means they are also prone to vivid and scary nightmares. Again, choose stories wisely for bedtime.

*Parent Traps:*

- Interfering when Little Learners are working to figure something out. They are proud of their independence, and want to show you that they can do it themselves. They will ask for help when they need it.
- Showing frustration with Little Learners when they are exploring and taking things apart. They are not doing it to frustrate you, this is how they find out about their world.

*Parent Tips:*

- Allow Little Learners to experiment for themselves, provide opportunities where they can enjoy finding their own answers to 'why'. Be patient when they want to experiment. If they are interested in the light switch then find an old one and let them take it to pieces.
- Although they want to do things independently, remember it is important to be there when they do ask for help. Also, whilst they don't need as much praise as some others, such as Little Helpers, they do welcome encouragement to know they are on the right track.
- Provide logical reasons for any rules you want them to follow, and make sure your reprimands are reasonable. This will mean your Little Learner respects your decisions.

## Learner Jenny

"Jenny is so independent and wants to do things differently from everyone else. She had a collection of rocks for a long time, and she would make up stories about where they all came from. She loves being read to, and now that she can read herself she can't get enough!"

**Learner Daniel**

"Daniel has always wanted to understand everything around him. We're sometimes astounded by how focused he is when he comes across something that interests him. He loves finding out all its possible functions (maybe even inventing new ones!), and he quickly became handy with tools so he could take things apart."

## A personal note

Parenting your child 'their way' doesn't mean you have to abandon your own style and preferences. In fact, it's healthy for children to see that people operate in different ways. So mix it up, but when the going gets tough, think about matching your parenting style to what works best for them.

Using Personality Type makes 'seeing things through children's eyes' even more fun and interesting. For me, it has brought out how all their unique differences and wonderful qualities make a very colourful world indeed. By truly understanding their needs, quirks and how they prefer to be in their world, we can help them become the best version of themselves that they can be. When we show acceptance, understanding and support for how they do things and how they feel, we are building their self-esteem and their confidence. They are not mini versions of us, but mini versions of themselves, and we're supporting them in happily developing into genuine, authentic and rounded individuals.

Now when I look in the mirror I see a more content face. I may still look tired, but most certainly content. The Soul Guide in me is basking in all the possibilities, all the different ways I can handle situations differently, fine tune my parenting to my children's Personality Types, and get the best from each of them. At my best, I stop what I'm doing to really hear them. I look so I really see them. And I breathe. Breathe out the stress and frustration, breathe in the joy of the children. At my best

# :: Shopping Types

By Gareth English

## Introduction

As a psychologist I've been interested in the behaviour of customers for some time. I work with organisations to design their customer experiences, or to help in selecting and training their customer-facing staff. When we are doing this we draw from a number of fields, such as behavioural economics, the psychology of emotions and decision-making. However, I also find that alongside these approaches many clients can benefit from paying pay a lot more attention to the Psychological Types of their customers.

When I started out as a psychologist I worked under the impression that the understanding part was sufficient. If I understood my client and knew my subject matter then I'd be able to help them. So why didn't it always work? As I worked with more and more big businesses I discovered the massive importance of *how* you deliver your message. Being right simply isn't enough.

I learnt how to adapt my style to suit other people. I liked to put forward my ideas in a logical and confident manner and I was always ready to argue my case. It took me a long time to learn that this didn't work for everybody. In fact, I learnt that sometimes the harder I tried to show how competent I was, the less effective I turned out to be.

In this chapter I'll share some of the things that I've got right – how I've built strong relationships with customers. I'll also share what I've learnt from getting it wrong – the customers I've offended, or left uninterested, and the times when it hasn't worked out.

I'll look at a straightforward way to apply Personality Type to understanding what people are really looking for when they're

45

shopping. I'll also draw upon my work in training sales and customer service staff to help you consider how you can build trust and appeal to the different Types.

When it comes to making important decisions, then the middle two letters of your Personality Type are the most influential. So, for an ENTJ this will be N and T. You see, everybody needs to take in some information about what they're looking for – either by looking at specific facts (Sensing) or by considering the broader picture and what this really means (iNtuition). Then you need to evaluate this information to close to a decision, and here you use either logic and objectivity (Thinking) or your values and emotions (Feeling). This gives four possible options for any one person – ST, SF, NF or NT. To help consider this against the backdrop of making purchases, I think of these as four 'Shopping Types':

- ST – Researcher
- SF – Personal Shopper
- NF – Dreamer
- NT – Tester

In the next section of this chapter I'll tell you a little more about each of these Shopping Types. Then we'll take a look at how to really appeal to each of these before adding in a little about emotions.

What about the other letters? Where do Extraversion and Introversion or Judging and Perceiving come into play? These, of course, have an influence, but are much less critical than the middle two letters when it comes to making purchases. By sticking to these four Shopping Types I've found I have a system that I can apply myself when thinking how to put my message across, and also something that customer service and sales staff can easily remember when they're in the moment.

## The Researcher
(Personality Types – ISTJ, ISTP, ESTP, ESTJ)

Researchers are practical and logical people, who are straightforward and honest. So they naturally are looking for the same straightforward and honest approach when they are buying something.

When they are out shopping I find that they seek out value for money. This doesn't mean that they want what's cheapest, but they don't see why they should pay any more than they have to. As a result, they tend to do their homework first in order to discover where the best value lies, which is where the title of Researcher comes from.

With important purchases Researchers may even draw up a pros and cons list to make sure that they have made the most efficient choice. Researchers often tell me that this takes the form of a mental spreadsheet, where each of the options is evaluated against each of the key criteria. Many will say that for really key purchases they will draw up an actual spreadsheet, to the delight of other Researchers, and the surprise of other Shopping Types.

I have found that for less important items many Researchers will forego drawing up the full, 10-column spreadsheet in advance. However, they will still expect the salesperson to provide all the detailed information that they need in order to help them to make the decision.

When they have found a cafe or restaurant that delivers great value, they will tend to go back there rather than risk trying somewhere else that might offer worse value. They tell me that they particularly like it when the people who serve them are knowledgeable, professional and efficient.

Researchers make up around 36% of the UK general population.

### What makes them trust in a purchase?

Trust is critical to each of the Shopping Types. After all, the process of shopping means that we must have sufficient trust to make the purchasing decision. Ultimately, we are trusting ourselves that we are making the right decision, but that self-trust is going to be linked to the product we're looking at, the person we buy it from and the brand itself. Which of these sources of trust is most important to us will of course depend on our Shopping Type.

So what is it that allows Researchers to trust that they are making the right call on what to buy?

- *Knowing they've done their homework*
  Because they've checked out their subject thoroughly, Researchers can be confident that they are making the best decision, and that they haven't missed another option that offered better value for their money.

- *Listening to what established experts say*
  If they're not an expert themselves, then they will seek out the person who is. For example, when buying a new laptop, they talk to their IT-literate friend, or when looking at cars, they talk to their colleague who is really into his vehicles. Because they trust the person as an expert, they trust the advice and the subsequent decision.

- *Attending to the pros and cons*
  Since they've made a clear list of what is good and what is bad about a particular product Researchers know that they are making a mature, logical decision. It may be necessary to sacrifice some of the features that would be 'nice to have' if they are too expensive and don't add enough value for what is really needed.

## Type Tips

Those who are more familiar with Personality Type will recognise that what we're seeing in action is the information-gathering part of the Researchers personality (here, Sensing) that seeks out the detailed, practical information. This is supported by the decision-making part of their mind (in this case Thinking) that leads them to look for logical criteria to make their decision.

## A Researcher on a test drive

Sam (a Researcher) was out to buy a new car. He went into the dealer who welcomed him and started to show him around.

"I've already been reading up on the models actually", he said. "I'd like to take the XR3 for a test drive please". "OK", replied the dealer, a little nonplussed.

They got in the car and as they pulled out of the forecourt the car salesman said, "If you take a right here you can hit the main road and then you'll see what this car can really do!" To which Sam replied, "Actually no that's fine thanks. We'll head left."

"What's to the left?"

"The supermarket. I'm going to be using this car for my weekly shop, so I need to know that it will all fit in easily."

On they drove, Sam and the slightly put-out car salesman until they got to the supermarket. Sam then instructed him politely to wait whilst he went in and did a weekly shop. Once completed, he was able to see that he could indeed fit all the shopping into the back of the car, and that it was easy to load.

Pleased, he returned to the front seat. "OK", began the salesman, "so now shall we head back and talk finance?"

"One more stop", replied Sam. He then drove back to his house because he wanted to check that it was easy to remove the shopping from the back of the car and, of course, finally, that it would fit properly in the garage.

Only then was Sam happy to return to the salesman's office and complete his purchase, happy in the knowledge that he had checked all the practicalities.

> *Note:* Researchers like to do their homework, but there is also a key part of their Shopping Type that means they like to be able to touch and feel the product. They want to engage all five of their senses in the decision making process, to check that they've got everything covered.

## The Personal Shopper

Personality Types - ISFJ, ISFP, ESFP, ESFJ)

Personal Shoppers are down-to-earth and friendly people whose relationships with their family and friends are the most important things in their lives.

They tell me that getting great, personal service is really important to them and when they do get great service, they will recommend it to all their family and friends. However, if someone provides awful service, ignores them, or is rude then they will never return, no matter how good the bargains. In addition, they will tell everyone they know just how disappointing it was. When I'm talking to Personal Shoppers it doesn't take long to get some recommendations of somewhere or someone they like. Or to get cautionary tales of something that didn't work out, as you'll see in the next case study.

Because of this loyalty, Personal Shoppers tend to go back to cafes and restaurants where they know the people. They will say that it's particularly satisfying to be able to go into somewhere and have your order remembered, but it's even better to be greeted by name.

Personal Shoppers make up around 40% of the UK general population.

### *What makes them trust in a purchase?*

*   *The relationship*
    They have taken the time to get to know the salesperson, so they
    understand them. The Personal Shopper also feels that they are
    known and that the salesperson understands what they want.
    Once they feel that the person is genuine and they have found
    some common ground then the Personal Shopper can trust that
    they are buying from 'someone like me'.

*   *If they have been known and understood*
    The salesperson has got to know them. Asked about who they
    are and what is really important to them. As a result, the Personal
    Shopper knows that their needs have been fully understood and
    whatever product or service they are buying is going to suit them
    properly.

*   *The past experience they have with the sales person*
    Ideally they will have bought from this person before. They know
    that they were treated well before and so they can trust them again
    this time. If they haven't bought from this particular person or shop
    before, then they will have sought out recommendations, ideally
    from people they know well!

### *Type Tips*

You can see that the practicality of the information-gathering part of
their mind (here, Sensing) combines with their desire to make decisions
based upon values and harmony (their Feeling preference) to create
the need for real relationships with the people that they buy from.

## Disaster for a Personal Shopper

Patrick (a Personal Shopper) took his wife, Becky, and their friends out for a meal. They went round the corner to a pizza place that he'd been to before. He and his wife knew it as the pizza place with the blue door, or 'Blue Door Pizza'. They'd been a few times before!

However, this time it didn't go so well. They sat at their favourite table and ordered some drinks and waited to order food. However, the drinks didn't arrive and neither did someone to take their food order. Ten minutes later they managed to get the attention of a waiter, who brought them the drinks and took the order, although Patrick thought he could have been a bit more gracious about it considering how long they'd been waiting!

Things, however, went from bad to worse. After 45 minutes they still hadn't received any food. Again, they asked the waiter, who said that they were busy and asked them to be patient. Another 10 minutes went by and food arrived, but only for two of the people. It was a further 10 minutes until some more food arrived, but not the meal for his final guest. Patrick felt he had to say something. He told the waiter that they had come here many times before and that they were very disappointed. The waiter was not very apologetic, but he did bring out the final pizza and said that it was free. Patrick and his friends had shared the food as it arrived, so they decided to take the last pizza home in a box.

Once home, Becky popped the pizza in the fridge, thinking that they would eat it in the morning. However, when she went to make breakfast, she saw that the pizza was gone. Looking around the kitchen she saw no sign of it. It was only when she went to take out the rubbish that she noticed that the whole pizza box and pizza had been put straight in the bin. Patrick had come down in the night and thrown it away. There was no way that he was going to ever eat Blue Door Pizza again. Not even if it was free.

*Note:* Get it right and Personal Shoppers are incredibly loyal. Get it wrong and they will never come back. They will drive past your restaurant to buy more expensive food, that they don't enjoy as much, from somewhere else.

## The Dreamer
(Personality Types INFJ, INFP, ENFP, ENFJ)

Dreamers are sincere and respectful people, keen to ensure that they live a life in harmony with their values and beliefs.

I find that when Dreamers are out shopping, they want to be treated as individuals. They say that they are most interested in shops that are new or different and are looking for products or brands that they can identify with.

When they find something that is just 'them' then they are likely to buy without much more thought. After all, when you know it's right, it's right. Everything else will sort itself out. Because of this I find that Dreamers are the most spontaneous purchasers of all the Shopping Types. Just check out the case study of a Dreamer buying a new car.

When they are out and about they say that they are likely to seek out cafes and restaurants that are unique or special in some way. Because of this Dreamers often say that they are frustrated or bored by shops that are all the same, without any feeling of individual character.

Dreamers make up around 14% of the UK population.

## What makes them trust in a purchase?

- *The salesperson understands their vision*
  If the salesperson can 'tune in' to the vision of the dreamer, where they want to be and even who they want to be, then they must understand the Dreamer as an individual. They must understand that what the Dreamer needs is unique or different from the needs of others. This allows the Dreamer to trust them with the fulfilment of part of their dream.

- *The brand says something about them*
  Dreamers will connect with brands that speak to who they are, or who they would like to be. This will be particularly true when the brand connects with their values, whether these are values of individuality, environmentalism, the treatment of animals, personal growth or even indulgence.

- *The salesperson is sincere*
  They should speak from the heart so the Dreamer can trust them. If they need to be honest that something isn't right for the Dreamer, they will do so. If they say that something is a good purchase then that should be for the right reasons, not just to make a sale.

## Type Tips

Unlike the Researchers and Personal Shoppers, Dreamers use iNtuition to gather their information and we can see that coming out in their desire to focus on the future, the big picture and their vision. Because they use their values and desire for harmony to make decisions (Feeling) we see that the vision they are looking for is a personal one, where the meaning of the product, brand or shop is critical.

### Dream car for a Dreamer

Frankie (a Dreamer) was out for a drive when she noticed that her petrol was running a little low. She pulled into the petrol station and got out to fill up. As she stood, about to fill the tank, she looked around her. The petrol station was also a car showroom and there, in the nearby window, was an electric blue convertible sports car, shining in all its beauty in the morning light.

In fact, the morning light was shining in a way that meant Frankie herself was also reflected in the window. She was even reflected in such a way that it looked like she was sitting in the car. There was her reflection, her flame red hair flowing in the wind, contrasting beautifully with the electric blue car. Frankie was struck with a clear vision – this was the woman that she wanted to be. The woman there in the window. That woman was her dream of who she wanted to be.

Frankie said that she stopped filling up the car, walked into the showroom and bought the car. She'd sort the practicalities out later. Now she was a little closer to being her ideal self.

*Note:* When the vision fits, Dreamers are incredibly spontaneous. How could you settle for a compromise when there is the ideal? To some people this seems incredible, but I have heard from many Dreamers who have made large, spontaneous purchases just like this.

## The Tester
Personality Types INTJ, INTP, ENTP, ENTJ)

Testers are excited by new concepts and ideas. They enjoy examining or discussing options and possibilities.

I find that when they are shopping, they're interested in finding the newest and best options out there. They often tell me that they can quite often enjoy the 'game' of negotiating with salespeople and that they can respect a professional salesperson that does their job well.

Their name, Testers, comes from the fact that they will test the competence of salespeople and their products. Some Testers tell me about going to a shop with pre-prepared questions that they already know the answers to. That way they will know if the salesperson has got them right. If they do get it right then they can be trusted with the real questions that the Tester wants the answer to. The Tester can proceed, safe in the knowledge that this person knows what they're talking about.

On the flip side though, Testers say that they have no time whatsoever for incompetence. Should a salesperson get one of their questions wrong, or try to bluff when they don't know the answer, then Testers will go out of their way to avoid giving them a sale that they don't deserve. As we'll see in our next case study.

Testers make up around 10% of the UK population.

## *What makes them trust in a purchase?*

* *They've tested the salesperson. And they passed!*
  By asking testing questions, what they are really doing is
  establishing the competence of the salesperson. Once this person
  has they have passed the test questions, then the Tester can go
  ahead and ask the questions that they themselves don't know the
  answer to. They then know that they can trust that the answers to
  these questions are correct.

* *The product is the newest or best*
  If it's the latest thing or the newest model, then it must be the best,
  mustn't it? This can be applied at a broader level to certain brands
  too. Brands that are seen as innovative, or the best in their market
  will have a higher level of attraction to Testers, and they will be
  willing to pay the premium that such excellence requires.

* *Their own cleverness*
  Their own competence is very important to Testers, so they are
  looking for products or services that reflect that. Many Testers will
  say that they aren't sold to, instead, "I choose to buy". If they engage
  in the 'game' of negotiation Testers want to feel that they have
  somehow won. They will then trust that they have got a good deal.

## *Type Tips*

Like Dreamers, Testers like to take in information by considering
meanings and associations (iNtuition). However, their desire to process
decisions with logic and objectivity (Thinking) means that they are
searching for the best. This comes out in the product they choose and,
of course, the person selling it!

## A Testing test drive

Michael went out to buy a car. He'd done some homework on the model that he was most interested in, so when he got to the showroom he was already quite confident about what he was looking for. However, he played it relatively innocent with the salesperson.

"Hello sir", said the salesman that he met, "what are you looking for today?"

"I'm just browsing around", replied Michael, eying up the car that he'd been researching online before he arrived. "OK. Let me know if you'd like to know anything about this car", said the salesman.

"Actually I'd like to take this for a drive"

"Certainly, sir. I'll get the keys."

And out they went. As they were speeding along the main road, Michael turned to the salesman.

"So how efficient is this model?"

"Well sir, the whole range is very efficient."

"OK", replied Michael, after a pause, "I was thinking more precise information".

"Ahh. Yes. Umm 50, yes, 50 miles per gallon"

"OK", said Michael, sounding a little cautious. "Is that urban, extra-urban, or combined?"

"Erm...combined."

"Uh-huh. And what's the acceleration like?"

"Umm. 0-60 in about eight seconds, I think."

"OK. Thanks", said Michael curtly, "I think we'll head back now."

As they pulled up at the showroom, the salesman was feeling good. Michael clearly seemed interested and seemed to enjoy the car greatly.

"I'm going to buy this car", stated Michael, flatly. "But not from you."

Note: It's OK not to know information that Testers ask about. You can go and find it, or you can find someone who does know. Where this person went so badly wrong is that they pretended to know something that they clearly didn't. Big mistake for Testers. Massive.

## Making use of these differences

People I work with often ask me if I use this stuff all the time. I tell them the truth – of course I don't. Not in every situation. But I do make use of this understanding in a couple of key situations.

The first situation is when I'm looking to influence someone. What we're really looking to do in these situations is to build trust. So I'll remember how people like this person establish trust and make sure that I'm getting that right.

The second situation is when things aren't going right. For example, if I find that my natural style isn't quite clicking with someone. As a Tester, I like to prove my competence to people so they'll trust me (after all, that's what I'd want). So when things aren't going right, my natural tendency is to try even more to prove my competence. I try harder; I encourage them to ask me more difficult questions. However, this doesn't have the desired effect. If my natural style was going to work, it would have already done so. So, instead, the person I'm talking to starts to pull back from me (both mentally and physically). What I have learnt in these situations is instead to adapt my natural style, to try out some of the behaviours that other Types do so naturally and easily.

In the next section of this chapter I've collected what I've learnt from my experiences, as well as from people I've worked with and trained. Here is how to appeal to each of the Shopping Types, along with a couple of things that you should really, really avoid.

### How to appeal to a Researcher

Researchers are logical, objective people. So how should you present yourself to build trust and put across your point?

*Do*

- Be brief – give concise facts.
- Be straightforward and honest.
- Know the facts and expect to be questioned on them.
- Give information on the specific options so they can weigh them up.
- Present the information in a logical way – stay on topic.
- Give them factual written information about the situation.
- Have available relevant data for comparison and information.
- Expect to be questioned, even tested.
- Present a product comparison chart. They love to see the pros and cons of the available choices.

*Don't*

- Be overly personal. Don't share personal stories until they do.
- Talk long-term benefits before you've covered the immediate practicalities.

### How to appeal to a Personal Shopper

Personal Shoppers are practical and loyal, so what's the best way to build a trusting relationship?

*Do*

- Listen carefully to them. Give them your time and complete attention.
- Be warm and friendly.
- Give them factual information honestly, but with a personal touch – e.g. remember what they've already told you.
- Provide practical information and examples.
- Tell them about other people who have done it this way.
- Explain any options clearly and allow them time to decide.

*Don't*

- Forget their name.
- Pretend to be interested in them when you're not. Sincerity is key.

### How to appeal to a Dreamer

Dreamers have a view of how they would like the future to be. So how can you help them to trust *your* vision?

*Do*

- Treat them with respect – as a whole person with a unique perspective.
- Listen to and value their concerns.
- Provide overall solutions – an overview without details.
- Take time to discuss their concerns – be honest but kind.
- Recognise that that their situation is unique to them, even if you have seen something very similar before.
- Be sincere.
- Get to know them as a person.
- If they wish to discuss alternatives, take this seriously.

*Don't*

- Crush their dreams. If they've set their mind on something then it's probably best to let them have it.
- Make them feel like they're just another sausage in the sausage machine. They want to be recognised and treated as an individual.

## How to appeal to a Tester

Testers want competent products and services to be provided by competent people. So how can you prove that you're the person to work with them?

*Do*

- Respect their intelligence and need to understand.
- Demonstrate your competence.
- Answer their questions in an honest, open way – do not hide anything.
- Give them overall options so they can see a pattern.
- Be informed about new alternative developments.
- Do not expect or assume a personal relationship – that will be built when you've shown your competence.
- Show that you continually update your knowledge.
- Listen to their views – ask before giving advice.

*Don't*

- Pretend to know more than you do.
- Make them feel stupid.

## Emotions

We all know that emotions are key to how people work, but it's easy to overlook just how important our emotions are when it comes to decisions. Of course the decisions that we make as customers are no exception to this. Many of us would like to think that we're rational when it comes to making decisions. The truth though is that the emotional part of our brain has a massive impact for all of us. Yes, even Researchers and Testers with their Thinking Preferences! Humans are wired to want to avoid some emotions, like feeling sad or angry. We're also wired to seek out other positive feelings, like being happy or loved. However, we also know that personality plays a key part here – not everyone views the same emotions in the same way. For example, some people hate being scared, whilst other people give up good time and money to go to scary movies. We're wired up in slightly different ways.

In fact, we can take this further and think of all the things we buy: products, services, ideas, as helping us to feel certain emotions, or to avoid others. For example, I'm feeling insecure in my home so I buy an alarm. I'm feeling underappreciated so I buy something to treat myself.

When looking at building better customer experiences, Personality Type can help us out by letting us think in more detail about which emotions certain people want to feel or avoid.

# Researchers

| Avoid | Desire |
|-------|--------|
| • Fear | • Safety |
| • Insecurity | • Relief |
| • Envy | • Satisfaction |

# Personal Shoppers

| Avoid | Desire |
|---|---|
| • Rejection<br>• Loneliness<br>• Embarrassment | • Belonging<br>• Love<br>• Affection |

# Dreamers

| Avoid | Desire |
|---|---|
| • Boredom<br>• Unhappiness<br>• Monotony | • Surprise<br>• Wonder<br>• Pride |

# Testers

| Avoid | Desire |
|---|---|
| • Envy<br>• Boredom<br>• Incompetence | • Pride in their achievement<br>• Satisfaction<br>• Excitement |

If we keep these 'Avoid' and 'Desire' emotions in mind then we know a little more about what these Shopping Types are doing, and what they're trying to achieve when they make purchases. You know that if you do anything that makes a Personal Shopper feel rejected, then they're going to react. Probably by buying somewhere else next time, and telling everyone else to avoid you. On the other hand, if you can make them feel a sense of belonging, or even loved, then they're going to be delighted and they'll seek you out when they want to feel competent again.

## Business to business

The simplest way to observe these Shopping Types is when people are out buying something for themselves – cars, muffins, computers or a cup of coffee. However, we also know that these same preferences are at play when people buy and sell ideas or services into businesses.

In fact, you've probably seen some of these Shopping Types if you've ever sold business to business. Or even if you've presented to other departments in a large company – the Researchers want detailed questions, whilst the Testers start challenging your competence to see if you can stand up for yourself.

So you can apply the same principles to understanding what someone's Shopping Style is. You might want to think of it as a Buying Style or Influencing Style at work, but the same principles of Personality Type and emotions are at play.

## Conclusion

We have looked here at how Personality Type can be applied to the retail experience to give us the four Shopping Types. We've seen they can be similar. After all, we all want Trust. And we've seen their differences – what brings us to trust depends on who we are.

We've also looked at how to appeal to each of these Types, what works for them and what you can do that will really put them off. We've even looked beneath the surface to consider what emotions they really want to feel, and what emotions they are trying very hard to avoid.

Hopefully this has provided you with some insights into why you shop the way you do, and why people you know might behave very differently! It may even have given you some ideas how to work with your customers in a slightly different way to make them a little happier. I'll look forward to being one of those customers.

# Rachael Lewis

Rachael Lewis ran my original MBTI training, coming on for 15 years ago. I was impressed that she was able to bring her knowledge to life with such energy, wit and humour. This has been a model for me in the years since, both in Personality Type consulting and other work.

Well, those years have flown by and Rachael runs the highly successful Envision consulting company, who provide a broad range of services in both the private and public sector. One of the key areas that she consults on is the process of teams. In my experience, one of the great challenges of team working, and the reason that many teams are no better than the sum of their parts, is that they lack good processes for making decisions. One of the reasons that I'm so pleased to have Rachael contributing a chapter here is that her works helps teams to overcome this problem and to realise the benefits of many minds.

Over the years I have often found myself holding up Rachael as a model of a truly effective ENTP. I share that Type myself and I'm well aware of the pitfalls, traps and tendencies to go rogue. I often find myself asking "How would Rachael approach this?" Well, today you have the opportunity to learn exactly how Rachael approaches her work with this very chapter.

Gareth

# :: Type & Decision Making–How many people can you get on a crate?

By Rachael Lewis

## Introduction

Ever had that feeling of being in a dilemma, when you have a decision to make, but you just keep ping-ponging between two options, or in a meeting, where everyone just keeps going around the houses by the same bus route, meeting after meeting, 'here we go again'?

Most of us have had this experience at home or work. Some of us have it every day with a particular meeting group that we are unfortunate enough to spend too much of our working time with. You know! It's that sinking feeling, as you realise the time of *that* meeting is approaching and you have the inevitable sense that it will just be a waste of time, *again!*

I worked with one team who, when asked to identify the most problematic decision they had to make, nominated the department Christmas do. Things had become so heated that conversations about the topic were avoided at all costs. There was no agreement and it was seen as a poisoned chalice as it was impossible to meet everyone's needs. In my experience we could just as easily be talking about office layout, who has which desk/office, parking spaces, tea and coffee facilities, duty rotas, and any of the myriad working decisions that groups and teams need to make on a regular basis.

When it comes to decision making, there is a useful model to use with Type that I have found particularly helpful. It helps people and teams to become 'unstuck' and move forwards with a very simple to use structure. Because it is simple to explain and use, you can pick it up and apply it straight away. It makes it easy to see where you are getting stuck with your decision making, or where you are missing important aspects for a well-rounded decision. It is also particularly powerful when looking at group or team dynamics in problem solving and decision making. It is called the ZigZag problem solving model and I have used it in one to one conversations as well as with teams. It is so simple and effective that, with some minor adjustments, you can easily use it with people who have no knowledge of Type.

In this chapter I will show you how I have used this model in a variety of settings and give you tips on how to use it to help teams to move towards making well rounded decisions. Although I have mostly used this model with groups and teams, it has just as much relevance in one to one coaching and personal use. At the end of the chapter I'll also give you some hints and tips to apply the ZigZag model to your own decision making.

## The Christmas party

Working with a public relations team highlighted the usefulness of ZigZag as a process. I invited them to bring along a particularly difficult business issue and they brought along the Christmas party. Other issues often raised are office reorganisations!

At the end of this process they did something they hadn't been able to achieve before – they came up with an action plan. Read on to find out how they did it!

### The ZigZag problem solving model

The ZigZag model helps to explore a problem or situation from perspectives that might ordinarily be missed because they relate to our less preferred ways of doing things. Type helps us to understand that we each have our own personal style and preferred ways of looking at situations. These are the ways that are described in our type description. However, this means that we often miss out on possibilities that are presented by our non-preferred style of doing things. When making a decision on our own we may neglect these areas altogether, unless we make a conscious effort to include them. Even when we work hard at our non-preferred areas, using them can be limited and exhausting, leading us to be easily distracted back into our preferred style.

In a group or a team this is exaggerated even more. If we have a group that is very similar in style and preferences, we may find it even harder to attend to the less preferred areas. This is because although we are individually able to flex our style, the likelihood of a whole group flexing at the same time is much less likely. Also, having people around who are inviting you to spend time in your preferred style is far too tempting and makes flexing out of style even more difficult to sustain than it usually is. This can simply compound the fact that we stick to the same perspective (as if the group colludes to pay less attention to our non-preferred areas).

Of course it is equally possible that we have diversity within the team. Theoretically this will give the group the ability to view the problem from lots of different angles. What often happens in reality is that this ends up as conflicting points of view that become entrenched and prevent us from moving forwards. This is where we get the feeling of discussions going round and round and never being fully resolved. When this happens, some people start to switch off and avoid getting involved in the discussions, whilst others try to continue to pull the decision back to their point of view. Two similarly determined individuals will cause a stalemate, or one doggedly determined individual will eventually grind the rest of the group down, until they get their point of view accepted regardless of whether it's the best one.

The four preferences that define our approach to problem solving and decision making (according to the ZigZag model) are Sensing (S), iNtuition (N), Thinking (T), and Feeling (F). In Type terms these are our 'mental functions'. However, as we will explore later the other parts of our Type also have an impact. The four mental functions are described below.

### Sensing (S)

When making decisions using Sensing we are relying on past experiences to inform us how to deal with new situations. We are concerned with the facts and defining what is happening right now. However, simply using Sensing may mean that we neglect to see the bigger picture or wider impact and miss opportunities or new options.

### iNtuition (N)

When using iNtuition we consider how this situation links to a wider perspective or longer term plan. We are concerned with possibilities in the future and may be inclined to adopt new or innovative ideas. However, simply using iNtuition may mean that we don't pay enough attention to the practical realities of the situation and may be unrealistic about resources and timescales.

### Thinking (T)

When using Thinking we are focusing on the problem, analysing what is wrong, and logically checking out the pros and cons of potential actions in an attempt to find the most logical and efficient solution. However, focusing solely on Thinking can mean that not enough attention is paid to how people involved will respond and feel about the solutions which can result in a lack of engagement and commitment when implementing actions.

### Feeling (F)

When using Feeling we are tuned into our own values and the values of others. We seek to appreciate what the impact is, or will be, on others and creating harmony and consensus is at the fore of our decision making. However if we only use Feeling we may neglect to confront the real problem in an attempt to avoid conflict or hurting others.

The ZigZag model moves us through each of these four perspectives in a structured way. This means that we spend an equal amount of time looking through the lens of that preference. This helps us to pay attention to all of these perspectives when problem solving and as a result means that individually or collectively, we are more likely to find the best solution. It results in more sound, well considered solutions and will also help to ease tensions that arise from having different types within groups and teams.

Figure 1 illustrates how the model advocates moving through the preferences in an orderly zigzag fashion, this is what gives the model its name.

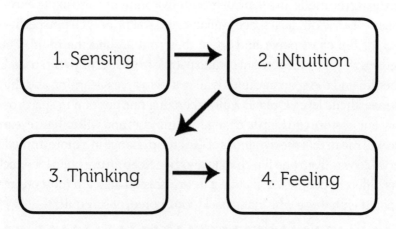

*Figure 1 The ZigZag approach to problem solving*

## How to use the ZigZag model

Using the model is relatively straightforward and doesn't always require an understanding of Type from your audience. With a little imagination it is easy to let go of the Type labels and start from the basic premise that there are four important perspectives or lenses required when making decisions. For example, Sensing can become 'define the problem as it really is'; iNtuition can become 'consider all the possibilities'; Thinking can become 'weigh the consequences of each option' and Feeling can become 'how does each option fit with my/our values?'

In a similar way to using the Edward DeBono Thinking Hats[1], for each of these lenses I have proposed a set of questions that will keep you or your group on track. These are shown in Figure 2. The trick here is to allocate an equal and specified amount of time (for example, five minutes) looking through each lens and to keep to that one lens during

---

1      de Bono, Edward (1985) *Six Thinking Hats: An Essential Approach to Business Management* Little, Brown, & Company

that time. You will be surprised how much of a challenge that can be in itself. When the time is up you move on to the next lens and so on.

If I am using the model in a team or group environment, I also like to encourage people to use the physical space available and so I print each perspective onto a piece of flip chart paper and space these out around the room. There is something very powerful about getting people to use the physical space. Using our bodies and the space around us allows us to access learning and thinking at a kinaesthetic level. Quite literally, changing our position in space, or even simply our posture can help to change our mindset and will enhance learning. It also will mean that the dynamics of the group change in a more immediately observable way from one flip chart to another. Keep an eye open for which flip charts different people stand closest to, are noisiest at, seem most engaged at, compared with those who 'hang back', look bored, or stay quiet.

## Group Facilitator Tip

Asking the group to freeze and notice where they are, who is contributing who isn't, and how they are feeling can give real insights to the group problem solving process. You can also allow the groups to stick post it notes onto the flipcharts to capture their responses and ideas to each question. This enables a direct comparison of the number of contributions per flip chart in the time given as a measure of how comfortable the group is at looking through this lens.

## 1:1 Coaching Tip

When working 1:1 with a coaching client pause after each set of questions and ask:
- How easy and enjoyable was attending to those questions?
- How confident do you feel of your answers and responses to that section?
- How much attention would you normally give to this set of questions when problem solving?

## And freeze!

I was working with a sales team at a global sportswear company. The team could not decide on their strategy for the next financial year. The manager was an ESTJ. I put up flip charts for each of the lenses and allowed 10 minutes at each. The first chart, S, the manager led the discussion and the answers fired up quickly. There were two Ns who stood quietly at the back of the group listening but not contributing. After 10 minutes I had to forcibly move the group on to the next chart, N. The group were slower to process the questions on this chart, but the two Ns moved up to the front and started to have a discussion about the wider strategy and economic context. After just three minutes, the ESTJ manager had wandered away and was on her phone. I asked the group to freeze at this point and observe the dynamics. The manager replied that she had estimated the 10 minutes at this flip chart must nearly be up so she had decided to quickly check her voice mail. Working on questions that did not relate to her preferences seemed to take longer and felt less enjoyable. This meant that as a team they were spending less time on these areas. They also undervalued the contributions of those who had different preferences. This had led to these members of the team feeling sidelined or undervalued. As a result they had either withdrawn or tried to stand up for their views but were seen as resistant. Using ZigZag it became clear that developing a strategy was something this group had the capacity to do well, but was currently not.

## Big tip

ZigZag is not about labelling or boxing people. It is about developing the awareness that we all add value in different ways and that we all need to have ownership of and pay attention to all the lenses when making decisions.

**S – Define the Problem** – as it really is!

Why do I need to make a decision/solve this problem? Why now?

What do I want to achieve in the short term?

What are the facts?

What have others done to resolve this or similar problems?

What has worked or not worked?

What resources are available?

What information do I still lack? How can I get it?

**N–Consider all the possibilities**

Brainstorm

*Don't leave out options because they seem impractical. Generate as many options as possible, you can evaluate them later. Ask question such as:*

What do I want to achieve in the long term?

What other ways are there to look at this?

What do the data imply?

What are the connections to larger issues or other people?

What theories address this kind of problem?

What are the possible ways to approach the problem?

How else can I achieve what I want? How else? And how else? Are these the only options?

**T – Weigh the consequences of each option**

*Do this in a detached and impersonal way. Analyse pros and cons.*

What are the pros and cons of each course of action?

What are the logical consequences of each?

What are the consequences of not acting or deciding?

What impact would deciding on each action have on other priorities?

Would this option apply equally and fairly to everyone?

What is the probability of success with each option?

**F – Weigh the options**

*This time, think about how each option fits with your values and the values of others. Use empathy to think about the impact on others.*

How does each option fit with my values?

How will the people involved be affected?

How will each option contribute to harmony and positive interactions?

How can I support people with this decision?

How do I feel about each option?

*Figure 2 Questions for each of the functional lenses*

## The Christmas party continued...

Remember the PR team we met earlier? Well here's how we helped them apply this...

Posters were placed in each corner of the room in order (Sensing, iNtuition, Thinking and Feeling). Each poster posed questions like the ones in Figure 2 above. The team spent the same amount of time (10 minutes) at each poster discussing the questions in relation to their Christmas do and noting down important points on post it notes. To ensure they did not spend too long on any one poster a stop watch and alarm was used to move them on when the time was up.

It was quickly very clear that some individuals were keen to participate at certain posters, while others became more engaged at a different poster. When the time was up, some moved away reluctantly whilst others jogged on to the next poster.

It was clear that the posters people enjoyed working at reflected the type of questions and contributions they usually made at team meetings. Below we will explore in more detail the impact of having people with similar types on team decision making. In this team there was a clear emphasis on attending to new possibilities (iNtuition), accompanied by being concerned for everyone getting along (Feeling). This was causing the team to focus only on the fact that no one solution could suit everyone's needs. Not wanting to risk upsetting anyone else, no-one was prepared to take charge and organise an event. Once they began to discuss some of the practical issues and analyse the pros and cons the team recognised that they were in fact not meeting anyone's needs by avoiding taking it forward.

The result was that they decided to run an event that had worked well previously (a lunchtime buffet in the office that everyone could attend) and also add an optional evening out for those who wanted, and were able, to take part.

## Learning Point

ZigZag helped them to see other aspects to the problem (Sensing and Thinking). As a result they were able to implement something that had worked in the past and recognise the logical conclusion that avoiding making a decision was not pleasing anyone. They explored the problem in a more rounded way and came up with a solution.

### Anticipating group or team behaviour – Analysing a team

| ISTJ | ISFJ ☺ | INFJ | INTJ ☺☺☺ |
|---|---|---|---|
| ISTP | ISFP | INFP | INTP |
| ESTP | ESFP | ENFP | ENTP |
| ESTJ ☺☺☺ | ESFJ | ENFJ | ENTJ |

In order to predict the strengths and weaknesses of a team or group in their decision making it is helpful to work out the team Type. This is the overall Personality Type of the team and it is calculated simply by looking at how many people have each of the letters. The most frequently occurring of each of the individual preference pairs is put together to make the team Type. As the adjacent example shows, it is entirely possible to have a team Type that doesn't have any members. This team has a team Type of ISTJ, yet when we look at the Type table we can see that there are no team members with the Type of ISTJ.

Once the team Type has been worked out the next important question is how alike are the team members to each other? That is, how closely related are their Types to each other, or how clustered together are their preferences?

### Working with Type alike teams

Type alike teams have a lot of overlap or similarity in the way that they function. In our Christmas party example above we saw how a similar team might collude and miss important aspects when decision making, which could hold them back.

Applying the principles of individual Type to predict the strengths and blind spots of the team Type works well with Type alike teams.

Our ISTJ team above, although lacking ISTJs, does have a lot of Thinking and Judging overlap with its team members and we might therefore expect to see them spending a lot of time wanting to make very logical decisions which solve problems. One result of this is that the team members may experience the team as having high levels of agreement or 'being on the same page'. They may find they are therefore able to move quickly to reach decisions.

*'We don't want any of those Introversion or Perceiving Types on this team, how would we get anything done?'* ENTJ Team Manager (Recruitment Agency).

However, they may find it difficult to move outside of their preferred lenses and may lack robustness in their decision making as a result. In our example, as the team emphasis is so strongly on Thinking, they are likely to overlook considering the impact of its decisions on those affected (Feeling) as can be seen in the case studies coming up later in this chapter.

### Working with Type diverse teams

Diverse teams are likely to experience difficulty reaching decisions because they will have tensions and conflicts resulting in their different approaches and perspectives. However, when they do reach an agreement it has the potential to be very well rounded and considered. They will, in effect, work their way through each of the lenses of the ZigZag although not always in that order.

Applying team type to a Type diverse team is less helpful as their dynamic is often around their difficulties in reaching agreement. Looking at our ISTJ example team there is some diversity around the use of Sensing and iNtuition as well as Extraversion and Introversion. This could mean that although there is a lot of agreement around making quick logical decisions, and high levels of logical challenge around the table, the team will balance the discussion of facts and previous experiences (Sensing) with a consideration for the wider implications and future possibilities (iNtuition). There may be times when the table feels divided between which of these types of information is more important to take into consideration and this could delay the decision making process.

## Using ZigZag with investment bankers

Several years ago, I was invited to spend a half day working with a group of investment bankers. The team was facing some morale issues and there was a lot of competitive behaviour between the members. The team leader wanted the team day to help pull them together as a team and to discuss how they made decisions as a team.

## Team Type ISTJ/INTJ

| ISTJ ☺☺☺☺ | ISFJ ☺ | INFJ | INTJ ☺☺☺ |
|---|---|---|---|
| ISTP | ISFP | INFP ☺ | INTP |
| ESTP | ESFP | ENFP | ENTP |
| ESTJ | ESFJ | ENFJ | ENTJ ☺ |

The team type was Introversion (I), Thinking (T), Judging (J) with an equal Sensing (S) and iNtuition (N) split. They were quite type alike, with only two of the 10 team members preferring Feeling (F)

I divided them into groups and asked them to consider the different functions on the ZigZag and how they saw them in action in their meetings. Initially, they were resistant to the exercise as, on the whole, they could not see the value of Feeling, let alone using it in a decision making process. The team view was that investment banking works solely on facts and logic with some strategic thinking. However, they eventually complied due to the predominance of Judging (J) in the group who wanted to follow the agenda and plan.

The outcome of this activity was very powerful. The Feeling preference team members raised their awareness of the lack of motivation and team spirit. They identified that Feeling wasn't incorporated into decision making and this impacted on the team's lack of attention to supporting its own members. Initially the rest of the team argued against this position. However, the ISFJ was able to provide compelling facts backed up with real examples that supported this assertion (how many people had left the team, the number of people who did not attend weekly meetings, and the reputation of the team with other teams in the business).

Whilst the team members contemplated this compelling case, the INFP was also able to add that not only did the lack of Feeling impact on the internal performance of the team, but that it had also led to a serious error of judgment about an investment decision which had lost them lots of money. You may recall the controversial Benetton advertising campaign which impacted significantly on the company's market share and share prices. This team had not considered the values of Benetton, or the strength of feeling or values of the public in relation to the adverts.

## Learning point

The team began to see the logical impact of using Feeling in their decision making. They began to consider how they might use this preference to better effect when making decisions in future. They agreed that when investigating potential investments they could improve those decisions by considering the target organisation's values towards its employees; as it is sustaining people's performance that determines how well a company makes a return on the investment.

### Helping groups and teams to make better decisions

Often, with a team or a group, I will get them to come along with a predetermined decision that they want to move forward with, but are finding hard to reach a solution or conclusion about. Many groups bring issues that they have been debating for weeks, even months, and are surprised at how the ZigZag model can help them to reach a decision within an hour.

The example below shows how I used it to work with a community mental health team who had an unresolved problem with their on-duty rota which was causing friction with the office staff.

## On-duty rota in a community mental health team

| | | | |
|---|---|---|---|
| ISTJ | ISFJ | INFJ | INTJ |
| ISTP ☺ | ISFP | INFP | INTP ☺ |
| ESTP ☺ | ESFP | ENFP | ENTP ☺☺☺ |
| ESTJ | ESFJ ☺ | ENFJ | ENTJ ☺ |

The team type was ENTP. Although the team had some diversity it only had one F preference.

As a team they identified that they were strong at dealing with change and being resourceful with financial constraints. They felt they were approachable with lots of expertise in the team and that they were generally well informed. However, they could do with tightening up on procedures and had real problems manning the on-duty rota that had been drawn up to ensure that there was an expert in the office to support the office staff when taking emergency calls. However, in reality they were finding it impossible to meet the demands of their roles and fulfil their turn on duty. As a result, the on-duty rota was not being followed and there was increasing tension with the office/administration staff who felt that they were left to back fill the rota when they were not qualified.

Using the questions given in Figure 2, I moved them around a series of posters within the room. The first stop was Sensing and they were to spend 10 minutes answering the questions on this poster. They were not allowed to deviate outside of Sensing questions or move on before the 10 minutes was up. It was immediately obvious that two of the quieter members of the team were leading this discussion (ISFJ and ISTP). 'We need on duty cover to deal with calls; there are eight of us; we each have x cases to manage...' Several of the Ns looked at their watches throughout and showed signs of disengagement with the activity.

After exactly 10 minutes they moved along to iNtuition poster with questions. The rules remained the same. The energy in those with an iNtuitive (N) preference rose and they began to engage with a discussion about the questions, those with a Sensing preference (S) tried to join in but, after a couple of minutes, exhausted their energy and started to look around the room for some distractions. 'There are resourcing cuts across the service; it links to an increase in workload demand; the government is changing direction...'

Before moving on the next flip chart we reviewed the activity so far. People easily recognised how well they engaged at each flip chart and found it hard to believe that there had only/already been 10 minutes at each one. What came to light was that although the Sensing (S) preferences were in a minority, in team discussions their views were listened to and not sidelined. We moved on to the Thinking (T) Poster. There was an energetic analysis of the problem, almost everyone engaged listing the problems and the pros and cons of possible solutions. 'If we change the rota to include.... the problem is....' 'It would make logical sense to....' flew around the room, apart from the one person with a Feeling (F) preference, who stood just outside the group and listened intently. It was hard to move the group on after the 10 minutes. They were energetic and engaged, but no clearer on a solution.

Finally, I moved them on to the Feeling (F) flip chart. The room fell silent, people shuffled, looked at their feet, and scratched their heads. They stood apart in a wide space away from the flip chart, like teenagers hanging out around a street corner. Finally, after about seven minutes of no-one talking, the person with the Feeling preference (F) said, 'I suppose the real problem isn't that there is someone on duty, it is how the office staff feel when they get an emergency call. They don't feel confident enough to take it, and they just want the support of an expert to help them'. It was like a penny dropping. Looking at the problem through this lens meant that they did not actually need an on-duty rota that conflicted with their case loads, but that they needed to pay more attention to the needs and feelings of the office staff in order to build their confidence that support was available when they needed it.

### Learning point

The problem wasn't that they couldn't find the answer, the problem had been that as a group they normally felt so uncomfortable looking through the Feeling lens that they glossed over it and moved back to Thinking whenever possible. They were only seeing half the situation. Once they managed to see the situation as it really was, the solution was simple and achievable.

## *Moving to a Decision*

Once the team has discussed the issues using the four lenses it is time to move towards a decision. To do this I simply allow 10 to 20 minutes at the end of the ZigZag process to allow the group to pull their thoughts together and come up with an action plan.

### *Facilitator Tip*

I use the questions in Figure 3 to help give some structure to this part of the process.

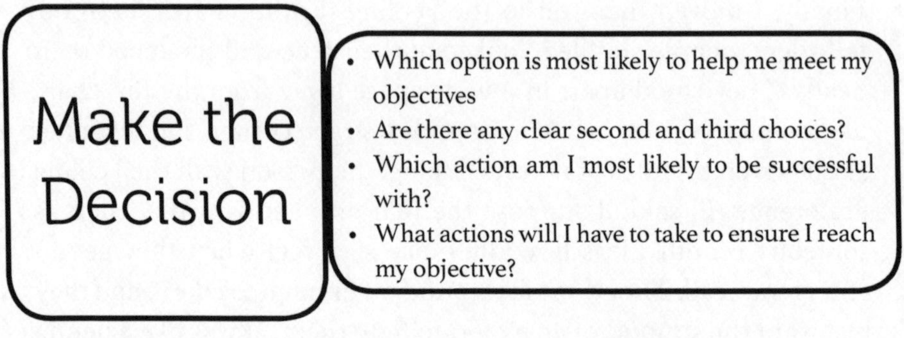
Make the Decision
• Which option is most likely to help me meet my objectives
• Are there any clear second and third choices?
• Which action am I most likely to be successful with?
• What actions will I have to take to ensure I reach my objective?

*Figure 3 Suggested structure to reach closure on the ZigZag decision*

## Facilitator Tip: Working with very large groups or teams

If you are working with a very large group (usually more than eight people) you could try putting people into smaller working groups which reflect the teams the typically work in on a day to day basis. This can be very insightful where you have teams with different cultures such as Marketing and Finance.

If you are working with a group on a development programme (who do not work together normally as a team) you can split them into Type alike groups (ST, NT, SF and NF) to compare and contrast the way they function and make decisions. You can see from the example below how this worked very effectively when I used it with a group of GPs on an outward bound development programme.

### Type alike teams of GPs on an outward bound course

This group of 24 or so GPs was split into three groups. We had one group which was made up of Sensing and Thinking (ST) types; one group of iNtuition and Feeling (NF) types, and a mixed group of Sensing Feeling (SF) and iNtuition and Thinking (NT) types.

Each team was given a series of outdoor activities and puzzles to solve. When they had completed them they were given a list of statements which described ST, NT, SF, and NF approaches to problem solving and team working. The group were asked to select the top five statements that best described how they had worked together and the bottom five statements that least described how they worked together.

The ST team described their approach as focused on solving the problem in the most efficient way possible and having a clear straight forward style. But they did not consider themselves to be concerned with team members having a getting along well or everyone feeling valued for their input.

The NF team described themselves as being concerned that everyone got along well and ensuring all team members felt valued for their input. But they did not consider themselves to be concerned with focusing on the most efficient way to solve the problem possible, or having a clear and straight forward style.

When they shared these approaches the ST team accused the NF team of 'faffing around and not getting on with solving the problems'. The NF team responded by saying they had had a lovely time together and had lots of fun and as a result they felt very bonded. The ST team replied that they could not believe that it was fun if you hadn't solved all the puzzles in the quickest possible time.

In contrast, the mixed SF and NT team said that they couldn't agree on just five statements as they had felt they were very different in their approaches, but that they felt they had made some excellent decisions listening to all the different perspectives.

### Key learning point

As we discussed earlier, teams that have similar membership tend to agree quickly, but miss some of the important aspects when making decisions (see the ST and NF teams above), whereas teams that are very different and diverse can find that communication takes longer, but that when they make a decision it is well-rounded and considered.

### Extending the model further

When working with teams there may be situations when I want to add some further insights or depth to the ZigZag model. I have found that as ZigZag looks at Sensing, iNtuition, Thinking, and Feeling we can add some more sophistication to the model by considering the impact of Extraversion, Introversion, and Judging and Perceiving.

## Adding in Extraversion and Introversion

If there is a clear preference of the team for Extraversion and Introversion this may give us some clues as to which types of problems people or teams get distracted by and focus on the most.

*Extraversion* – distracted by the needs of those outside of the team or work group. For example, customers, wider organisation, family, friends, etc.

Teams who have a clear preference for Extraversion may be likely to over-focus on taking action quickly and relying on verbal agreements. They may be more attuned to meeting the demands of customers or external teams and will risk overlooking their internal structure or processes to meet those demands. In the crate example below we can see how the Extravert team jumps into action without thinking it through first.

*Introversion* – distracted by their own needs or those of people close to them. For example, how can I make this situation meet my needs, how can I get the information I need?

Teams who have a clear preference for Introversion may be likely to over-focus on committing to paper their processes and structures in manuals and written form. They may take a more considered approach and as a result can appear slow to take action. It may be that they neglect to communicate with others the decisions that they have reached once they have agreed on them internally. In the crate example, we can see how the Introvert teams thinks through its approach for some time before it takes any action.

## Adding in Judging and Percieving

Judging and Perceiving can give clues as to the speed that people or groups move through the process to reaching a decision.

*Judging* – move towards a decision at the first possible opportunity. Enjoy spending time on Thinking or Feeling but more impatient at Sensing or iNtuition.

Judging is all about reaching a conclusion or arriving at the destination. Teams and people with a clear preference for Judging want to reach that closure at the first possible opportunity. As a result they are likely to move as quickly as possible away from information gathering and will quickly evaluate options until they reach one that seems like a satisfactory solution. They will then move for closure (in ZigZag terms we call this 'going home').

For example and ESTJ team will review some factual details to help solve the problem and when the first solution that looks like it fits is found the team will go home. This can be seen in the behaviour of the ESTJ manager of the 'And freeze!' example above.

An INFJ team may look at some options and consider how everyone feels then go home.

*Perceiving* – want to explore as much information as possible before reaching a conclusion, may open up the discussion again even after an initial decision has been reached. Enjoy spending time on Sensing or iNtuition and will drift back there from Thinking or Feeling.

Perceiving is all about keeping options open until the last possible minute. People and teams with preferences for perceiving may give a lot of time to exploring all the relevant information and may keep revisiting new ways of doing things. They will discuss options and can have difficulty reaching closure and committing to a way forward. They may find that they keep coming back to the same issues time after time.

For example, the Christmas party example above is a very clear example of an ENFP team who could not reach agreement on what to do for the Christmas party. This was exacerbated by the fact that they wanted to do something new and innovative (N) and that met everyone's needs (F), which turned out not to be possible.

Below is a case study on how E and I plays out when groups have to make decisions quickly.

## How many people can you get on a crate?

*Simply using E and I to understand group decision making behaviour*

This example looks only at E and I in relation to the ways the groups behaved when having to make quick decisions. It aims to highlight how this can be used to add further understanding to the team behaviour when using the ZigZag. It relates to a group who did not know any of their preferences or Types.

I was invited to support a Leadership Development programme and offer some insights into how Type affects the ways in which we approach making decisions.

The first activity we undertook was to get participants into groups of Es and Is and give them a crate. Their challenge was to find a way of getting everyone in their group to stand on the crate. I was amazed at how such a simple exercise really helped to demonstrate type differences when problem solving.

Immediately the Es jumped onto the crate, some people fell off, everyone laughed, there were some raised voices as people tried to get their ideas heard. Still with some on the crate and some off, the Es then considered and discussed different approaches. Occasionally someone would unexpectedly just jump into action and have a go at a new idea, followed by bursts of laughter and joking. At one point there were two or three different strategies being tried at the same time. Bit by bit, they worked out what worked.

The Is, in contrast, stood for a moment in reflective silence. Still standing around the crate without moving, they then shared a number of different ideas and strategies and agreed on which they would try first, discussing how it might work or not. After a few minutes, someone stood on the crate and was joined by another. As they progressed, adding group members to the crate, they took time to review how their strategy was working and patiently discussed how they could adapt this effort until they got it right.

Both teams managed to get everyone on the crate and both teams had lots of fun doing so. What was observable was the process that they used was very different.

## Review

Es had a go (straight away), then thought about it, then had a go again.

- They didn't like to spend too long without taking action and their enjoyment and energy was easy to read as they were noisy and expressive.
- Their conversations and discussions seemed less ordered but when you listened they were quick to respond and pick up on the ideas of others.

Is thought about it and discussed it, then had a go, then thought about it again.

- They spent more time reflecting on how it might work before taking action and their enjoyment and energy was less easy to read.
- Their conversations and discussions appeared calm and considered, and when a new suggestion was made, they considered it carefully before taking it on board.

### Summary – How to use the ZigZag to improve your decision making

If you want to improve your decision making, the ZigZag model can help. Just follow these easy steps:

*1. Become aware of what you do naturally*
First, take some time to consider how long do you spend thinking about each of the different areas? Do you notice that is hard to sustain

your attention on one or more of them? Do you easily move back to a favourite area?

*2. Create a structured approach*
Give yourself the same amount of time to spend considering the four key stepping stones S, N, T, and F. Use the structure provided in Figure 2 to help you. Be disciplined and use a stopwatch, and make sure you don't get distracted. If you are really struggling with one of them, go and find someone who is good at that one and get their help.

*3. Balance J and P*
Make sure you balance the amount of time you spend information gathering with decision making. If you are a P, limit yourself to time spent information gathering, and give yourself permission not to make a decision in this time. But then be disciplined about moving forwards to making a decision when the time is up. If you are a J then make sure you spend enough time information gathering, hold off the urge to make a decision until the time is up.

*4. Balance E and I*
Make sure you spend as much time considering issues relating to you as much as you do those relating to others.

*5. Sense test your decision*
Once you have made your decision allow yourself some time to live with it before committing. Consider what support you will need to make it successful and what barriers you might find. Finally, make sure you reflect on how you feel about that decision having made it.

Of all the Type related models, I find the ZigZag one of the simplest and most effective to use with teams. It has the power to really help move teams forwards and can provide lots of fun and insights in the process and it really doesn't need an in-depth understanding of Type. The structure lends itself easily to being applied in everyday meetings and the teams I work feel that it is something they can take away from the session and continue to make use of in their everyday work. But perhaps, on a personal level, what I find most satisfying about it is that it helps everyone in the team to understand their value and the value of others.

# Rob Toomey

Although he is well known in the world of Psychological Type, I have only known Rob myself for the last year or so. In that time Rob has impressed me suitably that I was keen to have him join the other authors who I have known for much longer.

One of the first areas that connected Rob and I, was our desire to improve the experience of people who were discovering and learning from Psychological Type. Furthermore, we both felt that technology provided powerful ways to enhance the experience without dehumanising it. Rob's success can be judged through his highly popular TypeCoach product which manages to make a more interactive personality questionnaire without compromising on quality.

Rob is also clearly outspoken in his view that the Type community needs to do more to engage with current and future clients, a concept very close to my heart. Rob has spoken many times about the need for Psychological Type to be both accessible and powerful if it is to add value and it is this very topic that is the subject of his chapter here.

Gareth

# :: The Value of Type

By Rob Toomey

## Introduction

Twenty years ago, my wife Carly and I began talking about Personality Type. Over time, our interest and energy for the topic has continued to grow – the more we learn and observe, the more fascinated we become and the more value we see that Type can deliver. I do not believe there is a better vehicle to observe, understand and change human behavior. Eleven years ago, I left my career as an attorney and Carly left her career as a teacher to start a business focused on the applications of Personality Type. I feel extraordinarily grateful that our passion for this subject allows us to spend most of our waking hours devoted to helping others achieve more professionally and personally based on these insights.

And yet, despite how obvious the value of these insights is to me, every day I am tasked with explaining *why* Personality Type is valuable. I've learned that it's not obvious to busy leaders who are disciplined in making sure that they spend their resources in the most effective manner. With shareholders and board members reviewing their every move, they are right to ask tough questions about the value Type can have for their organisation.

This chapter presents an impassioned argument in favor of using Personality Type. I hope this will benefit leaders who wonder what Type can do for the performance of their organisation as well as individuals who are curious about the range of impacts Type can have. I have not witnessed a more powerful way for individual and organisations to achieve their goals than Personality Type. The evidence from clients is clear – when teams and leaders properly incorporate an understanding of Type principles into their interactions with others, they see compelling results. Below, I've laid out the kinds of impact Type can have and also the best practices in terms of *how* to actually do it.

## But first, a story

Michael is an associate with one of our largest clients. His job is to travel the world, buying great products that will eventually go into his employer's stores. Like all of his colleagues, Michael has experienced extensive training on communication, influence and negotiation skills that heavily incorporate Personality Type principles. He is adept at identifying the Personality Type and communication style of others and has honed the skill of adjusting his approach to create the highest likelihood of understanding.

Michael had just arrived in New York City and hadn't slept well on the flight from London. He and his boss, Liz, were zooming across Manhattan in the back of a taxi for a lunch meeting with a key supplier. Michael has had had limited interactions with the supplier. Fortunately, Liz had been in the business for more than 20 years and had worked with Henri extensively.

Scanning her phone for last minute emails, Liz explained "Henri is French through and through. Although he's lived in the US for almost 20, he very much appreciates even small gestures to acknowledge his French background. Lunch will be long, we will let him bring up the business, and please make sure to mention how much you enjoyed the food as his uncle owns the restaurant."

"Sounds good", Michael thought, the food would probably help his jet lag.

Liz continued, "I'm pretty sure that Henri is an ENTJ. Direct, bold and logical – our relationship with his firm has been driven by Henri's conviction that we provide a valuable long-term strategic partnership opportunity. He's made a number of short-term sacrifices towards that vision. It's critical when we explain the plans for the upcoming season that he sees how it fits into his 5-year plan."

Michael started to chew on this information. It had taken a while for him to appreciate that some ENTJs enjoyed debating in order to understand his thinking (not as a sign of disagreement). But he'd built up his ability to be assertive and now felt confident with those conversations. Michael then reasoned that Henri's French background would have likely magnified some of the natural tendencies of the ENTJ. He was glad Liz had shared this information and headed into the meeting with a clear plan.

•  •  •  •  •  •  •  •  •  •  •  •  •  •  •  •  •  •

That evening, Michael and Liz raised a glass of champagne to celebrate the success of the meeting with Henri. As he reflected on it, there were two or three critical moments in the conversation where he and Liz had deliberately engaged Henri in a debate, allowing him to test and probe the proposed deal. They had focused on the long-term benefits to Henri, remained calm and assertive, and directly laid out the pros and cons related to their proposal. It was clear to Michael that the terms they reached with Henri were superior to what they would have got (if any) without framing the information in a way that Henri immediately resonated with and understood.

### Here are the client results I've seen Personality Type deliver

#### More deals

How valuable is it to be the first person called when an opportunity arises? In the case of the client in the story above, the stronger the relationship with a supplier, the greater the likelihood of receiving the all-important first phone call. Opportunities to get access to premium goods come directly out of strong relationships where communication is effective and trust is high. Our client's market representatives maintain some of the strongest relationships in the supplier community due to their ability to effectively communicate and connect with a wide range of personalities. By improving communication, deepening relationships and building trust most effectively, the client's reputation for being a go-to partner for doing deals increases across the whole market.

## Better terms

It's common to hear skeptical clients express that there's no shortcut to teaching the nuances of interpersonal communication and influence. To paraphrase, "It's taken me 20 years. There's no way to explain what I know to someone who doesn't have that experience." The truth is, much of the wisdom of the master communicators can indeed be taught by introducing the language of Type. Understanding a supplier's Personality Type provides insights into core values, motivators and allows the client's market representatives to tailor proposals and highlight outcomes that are most likely to resonate with the supplier. This leads to better-negotiated terms, usually for both parties. In addition, by communicating in the preferred style of the supplier, the negotiations themselves are conducted more smoothly and with fewer miscommunications and conflict, which, in turn, also leads to better terms.

## Improved team performance

Let's take an example. Most Extravert managers tell us that they need to improve their listening skills to get the most out of the Introverts they manage. And, because Introverts do their best thinking when provided time to reflect on a topic, Extravert managers can transform the level and quality of participation from the Introverts on the team simply by sending discussion items in advance of a meeting. Having a common and neutral language to describe basic differences among team members allows to communication to flow more effectively and teams achieve results in a more efficient manner. Further, a knowledge of the different activities people find naturally energising and interesting allows teams to divide responsibilities accordingly, which means more work is being done by the people who like that kind of assignment. Minor adjustments like this are precisely what allow the highest functioning teams to achieve superior results.

## Reduced work stress

A recent UK study[1] found that one of the top three reasons non-manual workers miss work is stress. In fact, it is the number one cause of long-

---

[1]    2014 Annual Survey Report of the Chartered Institute of Personnel and Development, 151 The Broadway, London SW19 1JQ UK

term absence for non-manual workers. So, what stresses people out at work? A closer look at the data shows that one of the most common sources of stress is poor work relationships – either an ineffective manager or just getting along badly with colleagues. Intuitively this makes sense – how often are the primary complaints from your friends and family about their work stress related to miscommunications, conflict and general incompatibilities with colleagues? Effective training programs based in Type improve communication, reduce conflict and contribute to lower stress. This then results in fewer missed days of work and a broader sense of health and wellness among the teams in the organisation.

## Greater diversity

Although still fairly rare, certain of our clients are beginning to appreciate that notions of diversity should encompass Personality Type difference in addition to traditional diversity elements, such as gender, ethnicity, age, etc. A team comprising an otherwise diverse-seeming group might still be comprised of very similar Types and therefore not have a diversity of perspective. A client of ours has trained thousands of their employees in Type principles and experienced a marked shift in how their culture now embraces and encourages the participation of those whose Personality Types are rare within the organisation. All of the benefits of having a diverse culture, such as more comprehensive and balanced decisions, more expansive and broader ideas and innovation, apply to Type diversity.

## Improved employee engagement and motivation

Why does employee engagement matter? Research from Gallup shows that companies with highly engaged workforces outperform their peers by 147% in earnings per share and realise:

- 41% fewer quality defects
- 48% fewer safety incidents
- 65% less turnover (low-turnover organisations)
- 25% less turnover (high-turnover organisations)
- 37% less absenteeism[2]

---

2   Gallup, State of the Global Workplace, 2013

The same research indicates that managers are primarily responsible for their employees' engagement levels. A manager who successfully connects and communicates with an employee has a huge role to play in the engagement level of the employee, which, in turn, materialises in the results above. Type training is the best resource I have seen to improve managers' ability to communicate with, connect with and motivate a wide range of personalities they are managing. In other words, Personality Type training for managers contributes directly to better employee engagement and drives organisational performance.

### Increased loyalty and retention

Keeping your best and brightest people requires providing them with work they find energising and which is in alignment with their natural strengths. Introducing Type principles allows for both the individual and his or her manager to ensure this occurs, which, in turn, reduces the likelihood the person will depart the organisation. Furthermore, many people leave good jobs due to interpersonal communication issues and related conflicts. By minimising these, fewer people are likely to leave.

### Achievement of key organisational goals

When you add up the specific impact areas described above and apply them to a large enough audience within an organisation, you see performance improvements at the organisational level. This might be increased revenue or profit for a corporation focused on those outcomes, more effective delivery of services and community outreach for a non-profit, and so on, depending on the nature of the organisation. Whatever the nature of the work, better results are achieved when communication levels are high, motivation and engagement is flourishing, and conflict and miscommunications are less frequent.

## The most effective ways of implementing such programs

### Multiple learning moments

In the same way you wouldn't try to learn a new language in one or two isolated moments, learning to apply Type principles requires multiple learning moments. My experience suggests at least three points of contact with the learning material are required and the more beyond that, the better. This typically involves:

- Offering a pre-work learning experience where the participants self-guide through key principles and have a chance to digest the material in advance.
- An in-person training program where participants ask questions from the pre-work and begin to apply the material to their own daily activities.
- Access to ongoing resources, ranging from desk references to online tools that further support the application of the materials.

All of our client work now leverages these best practices and the resulting impact is dramatically increased. In particular, the opportunity to leverage technology to provide ongoing support for months/years after a live session has the potential to allow organisations and individuals to continue to receive the benefits of their investment indefinitely.

### Focus on application

A great facilitator can only do so much – it's when the learner begins to use the Type terminology to articulate familiar experiences and synthesise strategies that the learning begins. By contrast, many Personality Type programs require the participant to understand a complex theoretical model prior to engaging in discussions around application. We have not found this to be effective. Instead, the sooner the conversation among participants can turn to real world applications the better.

### Escape the curse of knowledge

Type experts (like most experts) tend to speak about their topic using terminology and examples only other experts would understand. They also tend to focus on the most recent things they've learned. The result is the curse of knowledge – a language barrier for those seeking to learn a new topic. Overcoming the curse of knowledge is a lot of work. It requires building a step-by-step learning experience that assumes no grasp of common terms, concepts or examples. Often the work requires engaging a non-expert in the topic and testing and retesting whether newcomers to the topic are able to understand each step in the process. I also heartily recommend the book Made to Stick[3] by Chip and Dan Heath, which specifically addresses ways to overcome the curse of knowledge.

## Repeatability

Historically, one of the big challenges in the Personality Type field has been the wide spread of experience and related quality among qualified professionals. An expert with 10 to 15 years of intense use of the material with thousands of people is in a completely different place to deliver information than someone who has been recently certified. When introducing a topic as subtle and complex as Type, the quality of the facilitator has a huge effect on the learning experience. Thus, extra care needs to be taken to ensure a consistent and repeatable learning experience, which requires investing in the talent delivering the programs themselves.

## Scalability

Type training programs focused on just a top leadership team typically have limited impact on an organisation's overall performance. Really unlocking the value of Type means that training needs to extend below the senior levels within an organisation, ideally reaching a tipping point where the language and insights are widely known by employees. Since in-person training becomes expensive quickly, many of our clients look to technology for help. This might mean online learning that can be distributed across geographies and delivered down to multiple levels of management.

## Obvious strategic alignment

Most of our clients are highly disciplined about ensuring that there is a clear link between budget items and major strategic objectives. If a Type program is not seen as directly impacting the organisation's key goals, the support for the program will eventually falter. A great exercise to ensure alignment exists is to read the annual report or other key strategic

---

3   *Made to Stick: Why Some Ideas Survive and Others Die*, Chip & Dan Heath, Random House, 2007

documents of the organisation and see how easy it is to articulate the ways in which the learning program helps to achieve those key initiatives. While the value of Type and the link to strategic objectives might be obvious to the experts, it is not always obvious to busy leaders.

## Measurement

Economic cycles frequently force organisations to cut back dramatically on their training programs. Even excellent Type programs are discontinued simply because the value they delivered has not been properly measured. If leaders of an organisation don't understand the value the training offers, it will frequently succumb to budget pressures. And yet, extraordinarily, few organisations measure the impact of their training. It is reasonable to expect that the next economic crisis will yield similar results, with the exception of training that has been evaluated and measured. Ideally this measurement involves both subject survey of the training participants to measure their perceived results over time and a measurement of the objective performance of the organisation (profit, results, and other performance measures). We have recently partnered with one of our clients to measure both of these elements over the course of a one-year period with the involvement of a leading business school to ensure objectivity.

## Conclusion

The most common feedback we receive at the end of a training session with senior leaders is "Why didn't I have an opportunity to learn this material 20 years ago?" Personality Type isn't a magic wand that makes all problems disappear. However, it does explain the most frequent challenges that people face every day in their interactions with others. By introducing the principles of Type within a team or organisation, communication begins to occur at a higher level, conflict and tension reduce, ideas flow more freely, different perspectives are encouraged to participate, and ultimately the results described in this chapter are within reach. Bearing witness to the power that this material has to change behaviours and impact people on a personal and professional level is one of the greatest thrills I have experienced.

# Anna Crollick

I've worked with Anna many times over the last 15 years. She is respected by her clients for her integrity and dedication and I have always found her gentle insights to be thought-provoking, without being uncomfortable.

I still recall co-training a course with her that I was learning to facilitate. What sticks with me over the intervening decade or so is the way in which Anna used her great depth of knowledge and understanding. Whilst some people might be tempted to help themselves feel better or smarter by highlighting how much more they knew than their audience (and their co-trainer), Anna instead used her calm, thoughtful manner to help them to understand as much as they were ready to.

Nowadays, Anna runs Yellow Brick Road consulting, where she provides team-building and coaching services alongside her innovative new approaches to applying Type. Therefore I'm delighted that she has agreed to contribute this chapter where she will explore the fascinating links between Personality Type, art and music.

Gareth

# ❖A Creative Approach to Explore our Whole Self

By Anna Crollick

## Introduction

My first experience of the use of creativity to heal and calm the mind was when I was 14 years old. I felt like my life was in turmoil. My parents were getting divorced and my whole world view was changing into a darker landscape. I couldn't talk about what was happening – I just didn't want anyone to know. Things felt hard and gloomy and in my 14-year-old view, necessarily secret even from my closest friends. However, I loved my school art class. At one particular class I turned up feeling stressed and anxious. I sat down at the very detailed watercolour that I had been working on. It was of a skipping rope that I was painting with a really fine brush. Trying to capture every fibre of the rope in minute detail was 'doing my head in' and I found myself getting very frustrated, yet obsessed, with the detail. Luckily, the teacher came to my rescue. She seemed to instinctively know the best way to help. "Right, leave this", she instructed, and moved me over to an easel by the window. She handed me a box of pastels, and a massive piece of blue paper. Presenting me with a big coil of ships' rope from the art room cupboard to draw she said "OK, go big, No – Massive! Massive strokes!" Many moons later I can vividly recall this experience. The sick, panicky feeling of trying to paint the skipping rope and the uplifting, freeing joy of working in a quick, smudgy way with the pastels. I left the lesson feeling very different to when I had arrived. I felt renewed. Inside my head felt calm and expansive, and totally energised.

Now in my work as a coach and trainer of Personality workshops I try and incorporate the use of creativity to help shift mood states, understand problems more fully, and increase understanding of self and others.

On a personal level, I am always interested to see what more I can learn about myself through my painting and creative expression. I have long been certain that words are not the only way of communicating. What is most important and meaningful is that a person has a way of communicating their story in the world. Whether that be through a simple line drawing, music, dance, paint, mosaic, sculpture and so on.

Images can be very helpful as ways to summarise and 'see' a problem. I tend to use creative approaches in two distinct ways – either as drawings that emerge in the moment during the coaching conversation, or I designate a session to consider a coachee's specific issue using collage or other materials. Sometimes I offer the creation of a collage or image diary as homework. To give you an idea of how I use 'emergent drawing' here is an example with a client who I was coaching for leadership. I was struck by the energy and animation with which Bob (my coachee) spoke when he discussed ideas as it was in huge contrast to his energy for other topics, which was low and flat. Unless he was talking about an idea that he was interested in he appeared disengaged. To me, this was an important and noticeable experience of coaching him and I wanted to reflect this back and discuss how other people might also have this experience when working with him. He seemed to have little sense of how others saw him. I had a clear image in my head and thought I may as well share it. Drawing it out as a strong arrow with a kind of comic book explosion shape around the end of the arrow conveyed the force and vitality that I experienced when he was animated, as well as providing him with feedback from my perspective about how his impact altered depending on what he was discussing. It was a quick and direct focused approach that improved the quality of our coaching relationship.

I have found using diagrams and drawings as metaphors or explanations allows a creative discussion to flow. I often suggest that the coachee might find it easier to explain through a diagram or drawing, or we co-create an image that represents the key issue being discussed. From this perspective of being focused on the image some clients find it easier to be open as direct eye contact is broken and this can feel less pressured, freeing up the mind to 'see' the problem more clearly. Once it can be clearly 'seen' it can be more clearly understood and changed.

In this chapter, my intention is that you feel encouraged to try out a more creative approach in your work. I have added in some exercises that you can try on yourself and willing friends or family so that you can experience what it is like before applying to others. The key message here is that *creativity allows us access to new and greater understanding about ourselves.*

## A creative way to learn the dominant functions

Understanding ourselves is something that Personality Type is excellent at doing. So, what do I mean by the dominant functions? These are the eight core drivers that guide, energise and motivate each of the 16 Types. Each Type has one dominant function that is the driving force for them. It is the preference we use the most and have most interest in using in our daily lives.

Your dominant function is the core of who you are. You could think of it as the captain of your ship. Everyone of the same Type has the same dominant function. So every INTP has the same dominant function and every ESFJ has the same dominant function. We'll see what these are in a little bit.

Your dominant function will be one of the two middle letters of your Type – S, N, T or F.

It can be used in either the inner or the outer world. Some people use their dominant function on the inside. We call that 'introverting' it. Other people use their dominant function on the outside. We call that 'extraverting' it.

So, you have four possible functions (S,N,T or F) and each one could be used in two different worlds. That gives you eight possible options. – $S^i$, $S^e$, $N^i$, $N^e$, $T^i$, $T^e$, $F^i$ or and $F^e$.

If all this feels a little too complicated then don't worry, on the next page I've put a great table that tells you which dominant function your Type has, and some straightforward ways to understand what they're all about.

If you're a Type expert then you know that there's more than this in there, but you can get to that in time.

As a Type trainer, I always emphasise the value of knowing each Type's dominant function, or core driver to newly qualified practitioners. If you have this knowledge at your fingertips and can describe the behaviours, drivers and motivators for each Type, this will shift you up from being a competent to highly competent Type practitioner. People in a team event love it if you can describe what they are doing in terms of their core behaviours. They will instinctively recognise their description. For example, most ENFPs and some more playful ENTPs will recognise their Tigger-like tendencies (the bouncy tiger from Winnie the Pooh). The dominant functions come from the dynamics of Type, but we do not need to recap that here in order to learn the eight core dominants.

I worked with my fellow Type Practitioner, Dr Angelina Bennet, to design a way to help qualified MBTI practitioners reach that level of speedy mental access and recall of the dominants of each Type. We wanted to use a creative method as we knew this would enable both the speed of learning and recall. We came up with the following metaphors and represented them using a visual image.

| Dominant Function | Metaphor and Visual Image |
|---|---|
| ESTP, ESFP<br>Extraverted Sensing<br>($S^e$) | *Lightning*<br>Representing the speed and immediacy of action and energy and then it's over until the next 'now'. Having the space of the whole sky to appear in represents the value placed on personal freedom and their adaptability.<br>PEOPLE I KNOW LIKE THIS: |
| ISTJ, ISFJ<br>Introverted Sensing<br>($S^i$) | *Oak Tree*<br>Representing the well-rooted, stable embodiment of tradition and history. Each year is recorded and remembered within the tree by its rings, representing their vivid memory recall of the total sensory experience. They enjoy a stable and structured environment.<br>PEOPLE I KNOW LIKE THIS: |
| ENTP, ENFP<br>Extraverted iNtuition<br>($N^e$) | *Fireworks and searchlights*<br>Representing the excitement and immediate communication of a compelling vision. Flashes of inspiration and seeing the possibilities. The searchlights scan the sky for new ideas and highlight concepts of the future.<br>PEOPLE I KNOW LIKE THIS: |
| INTJ, INFJ<br>Introverted iNtuition<br>($N^i$) | *Spiral Galaxy*<br>Representing the complex inner world of connections and clusters of ideas, it is constantly growing and moving with new ideas held at the outer edge until they connect with the known and accepted theories at its core.<br>PEOPLE I KNOW LIKE THIS: |

| ESTJ, ENTJ<br>Extraverted Thinking<br>(T$^e$) | *Moving Sword*<br>Representing the sharp decisive action of cutting out what is not useful and getting a clear, masterful result. Using a sword well requires competence and responsibility, both characteristics that are highly valued.<br>PEOPLE I KNOW LIKE THIS: |
|---|---|
| ISTP, INTP<br>Introverted Thinking<br>(T$^i$) | *Oyster with a pearl*<br>Representing the inner energy for consistent working and refining of a problem to get to the prized pearl of a logical absolute truth. The more complex the problem the greater the enjoyment of the challenge for its own sake.<br>PEOPLE I KNOW LIKE THIS: |
| ESFJ, ENFJ<br>Extraverted Feeling<br>(F$^e$) | *Sunshine after rain*<br>Representing their personal warmth and pleasure at helping to brighten things up; having good personal relationships is very important. The sun is a powerful force and represents their passion and energy for sharing their strongly held values.<br>PEOPLE I KNOW LIKE THIS: |
| ISFP, INFP<br>Introverted Feeling<br>(F$^i$) | *Volcano*<br>Representing the natural wisdom and potential power contained within them. Most of the time the strength of their closely held values is not seen by the world, but their lives are guided by these value-based ideals. It is only when those values are crossed that there will be an eruption. This is in huge contrast to their usual dormant peaceful demeanour.<br>PEOPLE I KNOW LIKE THIS: |

*Table 1 Metaphors for the eight functions Copyright Bennet & Crollick (2009)*

## Exercise 1 *To help you learn the dominant functions*

In a team build or one-to-one feedback it is really helpful for people to have a description of the key drivers and behaviours associated with each Type, or for you to know those behaviours and drivers so that you can see them in action and then comment on how they are being used and received by others.

5.   Take time to read your own dominant function description above. Consider how it reflects the core of your personality and how it is experienced.

6.   Think of people you know a best-fit type for who are a classic fit of the description for each of the other dominant functions. Put their names in the spaces in the table. It really helps to recall and describe the features of each dominant function when you know a person who is a classic example.

I have found in a team-build situation this level of knowledge has been particularly useful at the Team Type stage, when all of the teams individual preferences are collated and discussed as one overall Team Type. Sometimes it can turn out that the Team Type is different from any of the individual team members Types. Hearing the behaviours of the Team Type is vital for the team to reflect on and discuss how they work together.

Another situation where knowing about the dominant functions is really useful is at the end of the feedback process when the client is deciding which Type is their Best-Fit Type. I have found that it is often the clincher when the client is unsure between two types that outwardly seem to have similar single preferences, for example, ENTP and ENTJ, that when the dominant is explained it makes the choice much clearer. So, in this example, I would be asking "which is the driver of your type? Is it about talking enthusiastically about new ideas, painting a picture of the future and always wanting to know about what is the latest and greatest, or is it about being decisive, achieving results in the quickest most logical way possible, cutting through the chaff?"

## Creativity using music

Building on the metaphors that describe the dominant functions, we wanted to help the Type practitioners to get a deeper understanding of the dominants by having a personal experience with each one. We felt that this would help people learn more about the dominants so that they could use them more effectively as well as allow more discussion between people in the workshop who actually held that dominant function. Also, it would provide an insight into how each of us experiences that dominant function, even though it is not our own. This taps into the Jungian theory that underpins Personality Type which says we all have the energies of each Type within us. How we experience each dominant function would give an insight into our own relationship with that preference and surface aspects about ourselves that we may only have been vaguely aware of. It would mean that we could express something about ourselves from eight different angles. This could be very useful in personal development work in terms of shedding light on how a person works as a whole.

Personally, I think it is really useful to know where our own blocks and positive or negative attitudes are with particular Types, in order to be aware of our own development needs as a person and practitioner. We all have them. You may already know your own Type irritants and soft spots. Below is a space to jot down your own personal attitudes. It may be interesting for you to compare and connect with any exercises you do later in the chapter. You could also use this with your own clients if you choose.

| Dominant function | Personal attitude (+/-) irritated or attracted | What is that about? |
|---|---|---|
| Extraverted Sensing (S$^e$) ESTP, ESFP | | |
| Introverted Sensing (S$^i$) ISTJ, ISFJ | | |
| Extraverted iNtuition ) (N$^e$) ENTP, ENFP | | |
| Introverted iNtuition (N$^i$) INTJ, INFJ | | |
| Extraverted Thinking (T$^e$) ESTJ, ENTJ | | |
| Introverted Thinking (T$^i$) ISTP, INTP | | |
| Extraverted Feeling (F$^e$) ESFJ, ENFJ | | |
| Introverted Feeling (F$^i$) ISFP, INFP | | |

Table 2  My attitude to each dominant

Thinking about this will provide you with information that might feed into personal development work, coaching or coaching supervision issues and themes.

Rather than just asking people "So, how do you use dominant extraverted Sensing?" which would probably just result in blankness, we used music as a cue, or prompt, to connect with each dominant function. Music is emotionally very powerful and evokes a rhythm and energy of its own that resonates with us. Finding the right songs took a while. It was especially important to capture the tone, energy and words that reflected the essence of each dominant. After many trials and errors, here is what we came up with:

| Dominant function | Types | Song and artist |
|---|---|---|
| Extraverted Sensing | ESTP, ESFP | *I'm Free* by The Who |
| Introverted Sensing | ISTJ, ISFJ | *Senses Working Overtime* by XTC |
| Extraverted Intuition | ENTP, ENFP | *Possibilities* by Josh Kyle |
| Introverted Intuition | INTJ, INFJ | *Windmills of Your Mind* by The Colourfield |
| Extraverted Thinking | ESTJ, ENTJ | *My Way* by Frank Sinatra |
| Introverted Thinking | ISTP, INTP | *Put it to the Test* by They Might Be Giants |
| Extraverted Feeling | ESFJ, ENFJ | *Reach Out and Touch* by Diana Ross |
| Introverted Feeling | ISFP, INFP | *I Ain't Moving* by Des'ree |

*Table 3  Music to engage the eight dominant functions*

### Exercise 2 Music and the dominant functions

Have a listen to the songs listed in Table 3, even if you know them already. You may want to compare whether you like or dislike them with your answers to Table 2.

With your Type expert hat on, can you see how they reflect the dominant function they represent?

To explain a bit about the thinking behind the song choice – the introverted Sensing song, Senses Working Overtime by XTC, for example, was chosen because the lyrics fit so well with what introverted Sensing ($S^i$) does and the way that it does it: "1,2,3,4,5... and I can see, hear, smell, touch, taste, senses working overtime ... trying to taste the difference between a lemon and lime ... pain and pleasure and the church bells softly chime". This reflects the detailed noticing of an entire experience. As well as this, it has a regular marching beat that reflects the step by step processing of introverted sensing. You can use these songs with a client or in a group workshop, but make sure that you can explain how each one relates to its dominant function. I find this exercise works best when you have a 'panel of experts' formation at the front of the group. That is, all the people who have the dominant function come out to the front when their song is played. Afterwards they can comment on how they relate to it and answer questions from the rest of the group about how they live with this dominant function. This is a great way to build understanding of difference. It gets away from a flat view of preferences, such as "All Ss like lots of detail".

### Exercise 3 Music and you

1. What music really appeals to you?
2. As you listen to your favourite music, notice its energy level – what is it like?
3. Can you connect it to a dominant function?
4. What is it that you like about the music? Is there anything you dislike?
5. What does it make you think and feel?
6. Notice how you react physically to the music, for example, are you relaxed/tense?

### Exercise 4 Music and you

Repeat Exercise 3 but with a song that you find irritating

This can be very illuminating if you have the chance to discuss in a coaching session as this connects more with the parts of us we don't like or accept. I have often thought it would be great just to have a whole coaching session where the coachee brings in and discusses a piece of music that they love or cannot stand.

### Bringing in the art – Creative expression in response to music

I was running a workshop for practitioners who wanted to know more about Type, and I invited delegates to connect with each of the dominant functions. The objectives were to learn more about each dominant as well as notice their own response to each of the eight dominant functions. I asked them to draw their response to the dominant function music in whatever way felt most meaningful to them using crayons or felt tips. You could use whatever medium you wanted, for example, modelling clay would be good.

As always with a creative approach, there are people who have had negative experiences with drawing and art making and feel uncomfortable with doing 'art'. It is useful to reassure in the setting up of these kind of exercises that their work will not be judged, they will not be asked to share or show it, although they can if they want. Anything that comes to mind is useful and interesting, even if it is words, or a line or a colour, reminding them that this is only about their response to the music and not about 'making a picture'. I actually don't say what dominant function the piece of music is reflecting until all the music has been played, so it is useful to either number the order of the pictures or have a system that works for you.

## Useful debrief questions

1. Looking at what you have drawn, do you think it reflects anything in particular?
2. What was your personal response to the music like?
3. Does this response connect to the particular dominant?
4. What does this mean to you in your daily life/work and how might this relate to your experience of that function
5. Are there any surprises here?

## Advanced coaching applications

6. Is there a metaphor, sub-personality or archetype that encapsulates this?
7. Does it connect to other coaching issues or themes?

In my experience, I have found that using this creative approach enables us to have a deeper connection to the personality. It highlights us from eight different viewpoints and allows us to see where positive and negative aspects co-exist and potentially how they are played out in the world. Through the use of music as a conduit to our personality we engage a dominant function and express this through the process of creating a drawing.

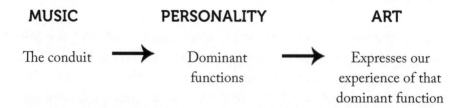

I have observed that when people are listening to their own dominant function their drawn images are typically very positive, represented by images that reflect a sense of home, comfort or strength and confidence. My own experience of drawing in response to my dominant function (N$^i$) song was very powerful. I felt compelled by the song, happy and strongly identified my own experience with it. It sounded gentle, magical and inspiring – totally compelling to an INFJ.

Interestingly, the same dominant function but in the opposite direction, such as Ne rather than Ni, often created negative images and responses for people. This fits with the theory that sometimes similar things that differ in a small way can be harder to deal with than things that are completely different. I have often observed this in group work with Type, the F$^i$s find the F$^e$s hard to believe and the F$^e$s find the F$^i$s 'not like Fs'. T$^e$s find the T$^i$s irritatingly slow and the T$^i$s find the T$^e$s lack depth, and so on, so it is not surprising that it came out in the responses. When I listened to N$^e$, which is my own dominant but in the opposite direction I found it a bit annoying, needlessly enthusiastic and hard to follow. However, on reflection, this was very useful for me to consider what a difference embracing the qualities of Ne would make to my life. Suddenly, I realised that bringing out my own enthusiasm about ideas with a bit more pizzazz would help my marketing no end.

There are no rights or wrongs with this exercise. It is interesting to hear from the group about their personal experiences to each piece of music and use this to inform their growing understanding of each dominant function and their unique relationship with it. Obviously, in a one-to-one setting there is more possibility to get into depth and explore more fully.

### Case study of Robert, ISFP

Robert, 40, worked for a busy IT consultancy and had requested coaching to help him be more organised and proactive. Whilst he was comfortable prioritising, his main struggle was with his strong tendency to procrastinate. He had taken the MBTI a few years ago and had a good understanding of his preferences and his Type. I experienced him as a gentle, friendly person that saw himself quite negatively but was struggling to make the changes that he wanted.

In previous coaching sessions Robert had talked about relationships with co-workers and had used Personality Type positively to help a tricky situation. He was at a loss to understand why he procrastinated, and was keen to learn more about himself using Type. Robert enjoyed music so I suggested doing the Dominant Function music and art exercise to explore the issue.

Having a real in-the-moment experience through which he could learn about himself seemed fun and he was keen not to tackle the negative procrastination head on as he found it frustrating and difficult. During the exercise he wasn't fazed by using the colours and used a mixture of imagery and words in his drawings. He chose different media – sometimes pencil crayons, and sometimes felt-tips.

### Dominant function introverted Feeling (F$^i$) – I ain't Movin' by Desiree

In the coaching session, lasting an hour and a half, Robert discovered several key things about himself using this approach. In response to his own dominant introverted Feeling function, he drew pictures and words that represented positive aspects of what was important to him. He described it as being about self-worth and deeply held values. The music itself made him think of another song by Bob Marley called *A Conscious Man*, which he said often came into his mind, but he didn't know why. He reflected that "somehow the sentiment is the same" and that making conscious choices about what was right according to his values was a really important. He agreed that this was a positive strength about himself. He also discussed that it was hard work to make his inner values external, but that was what he wanted to be able to do.

### *Auxiliary extraverted Sensing (Sᵉ) – I'm Free by The Who*

In response to his auxiliary function song for extraverted Sensing, Robert drew a very positive picture of a man flying through the sky with a smile on his face. He described that this connected to a sense of freedom and happiness and reported that of all the songs this was the one he liked best. It was interesting and unusual that he liked this more than his own dominant function song. We discussed what this might mean in connection to Robert's issue with procrastination. He realised that his values were strongly based on freedom of choice and that the Sᵉ helped encourage this sense of freedom and lightness and fun. For his own dominant function, Fⁱ, the freedom of choice was not about anarchy, it required "respect, understanding and love". It was clear that the Sᵉ could help bring lightness to the "hard work" that Robert had described in connection to his Fⁱ.

As we discussed the co-existence of the hard work of making the values live in the world with the in-the-moment, direct experience that auxiliary extraverted Sensing brought, we considered where the procrastination came from as these two aspects seemed, on the surface, to be very complementary. However, on deeper discussion of the images Robert had made, he talked about pull of the extraverted Sensing happiness of simply floating through the sky – "without a care in the world", loving freedom for its own sake. It struck me that perhaps the lure of the extraverted Sensing represents a "cheap fake version" of the sense of freedom, enticing Robert to experience the moment without the need for hard work that at some level he wants to do. I actually wasn't sure quite what I meant by this, but Robert connected with this immediately, acknowledging that he gets caught up in the moment but quickly feels bad as it is not "real freedom" and he is left with the empty feeling of operating without his core self. He felt the procrastination held his dominant hostage. This opened up the opportunity for a powerful dialogue between these two aspects of himself to explore how they worked and what they needed from each other to work in harmony. Drawing out the two aspects of himself as images made them more real and concrete and was revealing in itself. He drew out the values trapped in a bubble floating above the ground, occasionally the bubble bounced on the ground and the values were allowed some freedom, but never fully escaped from the bubble. It was interesting how quickly and easily Robert connected with this imagery and we used it in further coaching sessions, playing with the drawings and discussing how these aspects were working together as a 'temperature check' of his progress.

### Dominant introverted Sensing (S$^i$) – Senses working overtime by XTC

Another aspect of Robert that seemed very connected to the issue of procrastination was introverted Sensing (S$^i$) function. In response to the music, he drew a particularly negative picture of an angry-looking, shouting face with eyes narrowed and a jagged open mouth. The head was being bombarded with arrows and wiggly blue and red lines and bells jangling. He had written the words "dark and confused" because that was how he felt as he listened to the music. He described the energy of the song as harsh, "flinty", and that it felt "like being squashed down from outside, not wanting to engage", and that it was "shouty". It was interesting that as we discussed more about what introverted Sensing does, Robert talked about what it was like when he doesn't procrastinate. He recognised that to get himself going he is very critical and "shouty" towards himself and a lot of the time he is also critical afterwards in terms of "what took me so long to do that?!"

### Dominant introverted Thinking – Put it to the test by They Might Be Giants

Robert's most negative reaction came when we looked at his picture for T$^i$. He hadn't drawn an image for this one, in fact there was hardly anything on the page apart from a few words – "fun", "How do I know?" and "But really? How?" When I asked him about what this song was like for him, he said it sounded fun at first, but then quickly became boring and frustrating. He explained his reaction as intense annoyance at why people have to take things apart all the time, his biggest issue with it was about why people have to do this so much and that when he has to do this at work with sales people he really dislikes it "as it implies no trust". He was angry that it felt like it was never OK just to believe something. It was very interesting to explore how this conflicts with his dominant function F$^i$, which is the antithesis of the logical stripping apart of introverted Thinking in order to understand something. However, what was really interesting was that as we discussed this, Robert started to explore for himself how this could actually help his dominant introverted Feeling and that there was some room for this way of thinking.

I hope that this case study illustrates what can be gained by using a more creative approach to explore an issue. Rather than tackling Robert's lifelong issue by a more direct talking route, many avenues were opened up for exploration in future coaching sessions. It was fascinating to see how using the images and metaphors the issue could be more easily understood and how quickly we were able to access different aspects of Robert's personality.

In conclusion, I hope that the next time you consider, 'would a drawing help here?' you have the confidence to give a creative approach a try. Often, like my 14-year-old self, words are not enough to express the total picture of thoughts, feelings and senses. I firmly believe that we hold all the wisdom we need within us, we just need the curiosity, imagination and gentleness to allow it to see the light of day.

# Pauline Siddons

Unlike many of the contributors to this book, Pauline didn't start out as a psychologist. Instead, her original career was as a chemist. However, it didn't seem to hold enough of the one magical element that works for Pauline – people.

Well, chemistry's loss is management development's gain. Pauline is one of the most passionate Type experts that I've worked with, and I've seen time and again that her enthusiasm brushes off on her clients, who come away energised about their own potential and looking to unlock the potential of others.

Pauline is currently Training Manager at OPP Ltd, where she not only delivers MBTI training and consulting, but also works to design new products and training materials that will enable more people to get more from Type.

I'm delighted that Pauline has agreed to contribute her passion, knowledge and desire to share through this chapter. Here, she is going to be talking about one of her favourite topics – the impact of pressure and stress – and also making links to the in-depth areas of Type dynamics.

Gareth

# :: Managing Stress – The Power of Tent Pegs

By Pauline Siddons

## Life is stressful

There are some life events that are universal stressors. There are even scales which measure the stress intensity of each life event. Those that are considered most stressful all involve some type of loss, isolation or separation – death of a spouse or close family member, divorce or marital separation and imprisonment. Other less stressful events might be less dramatic but these are the ones that can insidiously conspire to creep up on us stealthily and eventually manage to push us over the edge, sometimes without us realising we were becoming stressed at all. Missing a deadline at work, dealing with conflict in relationships, financial worries or your daughter leaving all her A level notes on the school bus (or is that one saved just for me?). At our most resilient, we can take a few of these events in our stride and manage to get through stressful situations and bounce back, but if they remain unresolved and build up they can affect our performance at work, our balance in life and our very happiness.

## Tent pegs

It's sometimes useful to think about managing stress using an analogy of a tent in a strong wind. Each corner of the tent is strongly pegged down by important supports that keep the tent safe. One tent peg might be your family, another may be your job, the third might be your faith and the final corner might be your health. If something goes wrong in your life it's like one tent peg becoming loose and unreliable and the tent begins to flap about. The 'family' tent peg might get loose through family arguments or difficult relationships with extended family members; the 'job' tent peg might be loosened if there is a lot of change at work (or unpegged completely if you are made redundant). If this happens then the tent flaps around in the wind but the other three pegs keep the tent safely grounded. If two or more tent pegs become loose at the same time then the tent flaps around wildly and the wind can unpeg the whole thing and blow it away. The way to manage stress is either to hammer those loose pegs down by addressing the stressful situation or, if this isn't possible, we can rely on the strength of the other pegs to hold the tent in place by turning to them for support to get us through life's crises.

### Charity as a tent peg

When Sandra found out that her husband was having an affair she felt worthless and, as they headed for divorce, she became terrified that she wouldn't have enough to live off in the future after the settlement. She threw herself into voluntary work at a local homeless charity which gave her back her sense of worth and helped her to be grateful for the roof over her head and the ability to feed herself.

### Faith as a tent peg

When Mike's business started to go through the recession he started to attend church and found that the fellowship and support of others strengthened his Faith (and faith in God to be with him through the hard times). It gave him hope for the future of his business, and with that positive attitude (and he attests to answered prayer) he soon picked up some new work.

### Introduction to Type and tents

We can also apply Psychological Type to this analogy with each corner of the tent being one of our preferences. When we are able to use our preferred ways of doing things as we go about our daily life, then we are able to work within our comfort zone, we are able to 'be ourselves' and feel confident to stand firm in a high wind. If we are forced to use non-preferred behaviours then the tent pegs are loosened over time and the tent can flap wildly about making us feel over-extended, anxious, tired and stressed out. The great thing about Type is that it can predict the things that each of us might find stressful that aren't universally stressful for everyone. These are the things that others might find stimulating or actually enjoy, so they might not be so easy to identify.

## Something for the weekend?

Helen (ESTJ) enjoyed planning the family weekends with military precision as she was able to reduce her stress levels by planning when to get things done. John, her husband, (ENTP) on the other hand, preferred to leave things open and flexible. He actually found Helen's plans stressful as he felt pressured to stick to her rigid timetable. One weekend he announced that he had planned the family weekend himself and produced a blank piece of paper expecting Helen to feel relaxed as he had removed the pressure of accomplishing anything. It wasn't long before he found Helen secretly writing a list herself as she was stressed by not knowing if she would get her chores done by Monday.

When we are stressed by things that other people find energising it might seem to us that it is only ourselves that are affected by this. We may become self-pitying or angry or have an increasing sense that we ought to be able to cope. After all, other people are doing just fine in the same situations!

The beauty of Type is that, in describing your four Type preferences, you are describing four of your tent pegs which are your comforting ways of behaving. They also predict situations when these preferred behaviours are inappropriate to the situation and will therefore make us experience stress.

### *Extraversion and Introversion pegs*

Extraverts are naturally energised by external stimulation so if you are an Extravert it is important to spend some time each day either with other people or engaging in activities which draw your attention outwards. Extroverts become bored, listless and lonely without external stimulation so if your role involves working from home or being alone in a car for many hours, you can keep your Extravert tent peg secure by playing music (maybe even singing along), phoning friends to talk things through or joining social clubs in the evenings. When my office closed down and we were all made to work from home, only travelling to Head Office in London once a week, my home phone bill went through the roof! I found myself uncomfortable making decisions without consulting my colleagues, as I would normally shout across the office just to check what everyone thought. Eventually one of my introverted colleagues suggested we meet up once a week for a business lunch and that saved me a huge phone bill! The amount of time each person can tolerate alone will vary from person to person. Some Extraverts can only manage a few hours quietly alone but others can enjoy an occasional day away from other people.

The very same context that frustrates and tires out Extraverts – being alone – is a source of rejuvenation for Introverts. Introverted friends have told me how relaxing it is to have a week away at a 'retreat', spending time reflecting on important issues and focusing on recharging their batteries ready for the next foray into busy social situations. For Introverts, it is prolonged periods of interaction with others that are quite stressful, particularly if there is no opportunity for a quick break. My daughter once hid behind the sofa at her party for her 7th birthday. As always, I had invited her whole Primary School class round for games and party food. About halfway through I realised I hadn't seen her for some time so I looked around for her and asked her best friend if she had seen her. "Oh don't worry", was the wise response from her six-year-old friend, "She's just gone behind the sofa for a bit of peace and quiet. She'll join the party again soon." The whole birthday party ritual came crashing down on me a few years later when my daughter asked me why I insisted on organising parties that I myself would enjoy instead of letting herself have the party she wanted – one special friend for a sleepover. All the Type expertise in the world cannot prevent you from making major Type mistakes if you go through life on automatic pilot! Now she's a sassy 17-year-old, she just looks at me and says "duh! Introvert!" and points at herself whenever I force my own Extraversion preference onto her.

### Sensing and iNtuition pegs

People with a preference for Sensing will find security (rather than the devil) in the practical detail. Checking accuracy, whether in historic facts or present day reality, is something that Sensors can do to de-stress themselves in ambiguous situations. If you have a preference for Sensing then make sure you give yourself time to check your facts. This will reassure you and give you the confidence to trust yourself. If your job puts you in ambiguous positions where you have to make important decisions without being allowed to check out your facts then your Sensing tent peg will be loose and you will be anxious and worried about the decisions you make.

People who prefer iNtuition over Sensing will be drained if they have to check details. My father was very strict with grammar and so I became nit picky myself and people turn to me to grammar check their reports. I might have some skill in this area but, because my preference is for iNtuition and not Sensing, I find myself being dragged down into soporific mesmerism and have to take frequent breaks if I have to do a reliable job. Much more appealing is a nice creative project where there is little direction and a free rein to innovate – that is much more energising for me. If you have a preference for iNtuition and you are in a job that requires you to use Sensing then you can rebalance yourself by allowing your mind to free-wheel, either by reading fiction books, doing some creative hobby, such as photography, drawing or cooking, so your need for iNtuitive activity can be met and you can keep that tent peg firmly in place.

### Thinking and Feeling pegs

Thinkers become stressed out when they have to deal with emotionally charged situations. This might be managing an overly-emotional colleague or dealing with highly charged situations, such as difficult personal relationships, redundancy or disciplinary interviews. Thinking Types can usually neutralise these situations by giving themselves time to distance themselves from the issues and think through the logical decisions that need to be made before re-engaging with their empathetic side in the delivery of the solution rather than in the actual decision making process. If, instead, they are forced to make quick decisions in a highly charged situation then this will become very stressful. Mark (INTJ) is a very successful director who has a reputation for being an excellent 'people person.' People who have a Thinking preference can be great people managers – it's logical that people are important to a business and getting them onside makes great sense. A friend of mine recently referred to people behaving out of preference as "talking with an accent", which I rather liked. It isn't empathetic compassionate Feeling behaviour but is effective and skilful – like speaking Feeling fluently but still with a Thinking accent. It was only during the redundancy process, when conducting difficult interviews, that I noticed Mark's hands shaking and his lack of eye contact. He had been able to factor in the people 'stuff' using his Thinking decision-making style, but when the people issues became more and more emotional, he found it incredibly stressful and his Thinking tent peg became loosened.

Feeling Types, on the other hand, will be right at home in these situations and may even provoke reactions in order to be able to have some emotional content to deal with. I have heard Thinkers call people who prefer Feeling 'emotional vampires' when Feelers are expected to deal with issues in a calm, cold and calculated manner but cannot help but ask about people's beliefs and reactions to the situation. Feelers can secure their loose tent peg by sharing their feelings out of work with trusted friends while maintaining a cool business focus on the job.

### Judging and Perceiving pegs

We've all seen Judging Types sweating and panicking when an important deadline is approaching and they think they may not have enough time to meet it. It's impossible for Judgers to create more time in these situations and beating themselves up for not foreseeing unexpected tasks does nothing to help the situation. Judgers can secure their Judging tent peg by reminding themselves of progress they have made – the sense of closure will reassure them of what they have achieved. Concentrating on the important 80% that needs to be delivered can save them from the stress of tackling all 100% with no chance of success.

Perceivers, on the other hand, seem to thrive under tight time pressures but find working to rigid, steady plans exhausting. Perceivers are sometimes able to play the project management 'game' to keep people happy. When I was a research chemist, the management wanted us to plan which experiments we would conduct in the next quarter. My boss at the time, who is a highly creative ENFP, was always creating new polymers, but making him predict what work he would want to carry out in the next three months certainly didn't bring out the best in him. So we adopted a scheme whereby he would report to management a plan to conduct all the experiments he had already carried out in the last quarter. They would always agree with this plan, and then he was free to spend the next quarter taking his experiments wherever they might lead him. Management might have been suspicious that his progress was so predictable and so many of his blue sky ideas worked out, but both parties were happy so it seemed to work! A more rule-conscious approach, if you are a Perceiver, might be to loosely plan overall targets but still retain some flexibility in when deliverables are needed so you can maintain your control over choice.

## Advanced stress management

We've looked at the basics, which will give you some ideas about what will stress you and what will be sources of support for you, but Type does not stop at just predicting what activities each personality will find stressful. The tent pegs themselves have a ranking order with some pegs being bigger and sturdier than others. Carl Jung called your most relied-upon function your 'dominant function' as it dominates your personality. The dominant function is each tent's biggest and strongest tent peg. So why would it ever get loose? Well, humans are a peculiar bunch! Imagine an Englishman abroad. He speaks calmly to a non-English speaking shop keeper, "Please can you tell me how much this is?" The shopkeeper smiles in return and shakes his head as he doesn't understand. Persevering, the Englishman speaks more forcefully, stressing each syllable, "How much money is this?" The shopkeeper utters a sentence explaining that he speaks no English. The Englishman starts to lose his temper and shouts, still in English, "WHAT DOES THIS COST?" If he took a moment to think, maybe tried some words he knew in the shopkeeper's own language or took out some bank notes and waved them around he would get much further than exaggerating the very thing which wasn't working – communicating in English. When something we are doing doesn't work, we tend to fall back on what we trust and rely upon – like our mother tongue. With Type, we trust and rely upon our dominant function above all the others. The dominant function is the function which we usually have the most confidence and experience in using. Under stress, we tend to turn to our dominant function to help us out. Well, it has always been there for us before...

As we have already seen, some stressful situations are stressful particularly because they require us to use non-preferred behaviours. So, in the worst case scenario, when a situation demands that we competently use our inferior function (the opposite to the dominant and therefore our least trusted function), the worst thing we can do is to apply our tried and tested dominant function to that situation. The dominant function is the exact opposite of what that particular situation needs. When, unsurprisingly, it still doesn't work, we exaggerate it and keep going! It's like the biggest tent peg being constantly relied upon to keep the whole tent stable and being buffeted this way and that before becoming loose in spite of its size.

## At what time do we hug?

My sister is an ESTJ and when I go to stay with her she tries to organise the visit even before it's started. ESTJ's strongest tent peg is dominant extraverted Thinking which makes them excellent organisers and in her career as a teacher this has played to her strengths as she plans lessons and goes about the school day in a highly organised and timely fashion. Every minute of every school day is pre-planned, working steadily for each class to cover a predetermined syllabus sent out by the Examination Board. Imagine her distress when I refuse to tell her in advance what time I will arrive. I might want to leave timings open to see what the weather is like on the Friday night and maybe postpone the long drive until the next morning. But this means she cannot plan Friday's evening meal! Already feeling a little stressed and out of control, she then turns to her trusted dominant extraverted Thinking and tries to apply even more structure to the weekend – what activities will we do on the Saturday afternoon and evening and what time will I leave on the Sunday? When she realises I want to relax and adopt a much looser structure, instead of trying a different approach she starts micromanaging even more by planning what time we should leave to go shopping on the Saturday morning (and stating angrily at 9:10 a.m. on that morning that we are 10 minutes late and will never catch up! The concept of being late for shopping is not one I am familiar with but it doesn't seem to help when I point this out.). When her dominant function didn't work she felt stressed and turned to what she normally used to reduce her stress levels – being organised – which was, unfortunately, the very thing which wasn't working!

Allan, an ISTJ business manager found home finances stressful as some large expenses, such as car maintenance or home repairs, were impossible to predict. In response to receiving a larger than expected monthly outgoing bank statement he would pour over the detail, relying on his dominant introverted Sensing to help him out to make sense of it all. He would go further and further into the detail, analysing his itemised statement on why small amounts of money had been spent that month – why was the monthly food bill £10 more expensive that month? Which items could have been bought more cheaply? Where were all the receipts? Why had the car needed so much petrol? How many miles had he travelled that month? How did the fuel consumption compare with the previous month? All this delving into past detail might have felt comfortable to Allan, but that money had been spent and what was needed was a logical future plan to rebalance the account rather than wasting a whole weekend gathering data on past spending.

So if all our attention is on our dominant function pulling and tugging on our strongest tent peg, which of the other pegs could best save us? Our Inferior function is a good contender – after all, it is probably appropriate for the stressful situation in which we find ourselves. However, this is the least trusted of our functions and is therefore by name and nature inferior to the job in hand. Which tent peg is the one to save our tent from blowing completely away?

### *A little more complexity – and a bunch more answers*

There are eight possible dominant functions – Sensing, iNtuition, Thinking and Feeling and all four are possible in both Extraverted and Introverted attitudes, which makes eight altogether. Sensing and iNtuition are concerned about gathering information, whereas Thinking and Feeling are concerned about making decisions. So if your dominant function is Sensing (ISTJ, ISFJ, ESTP, ESFP) or iNtuition (INTJ, INFJ, ENTP, ENFP), then in stressful situations you are likely to start to gather more and more information either in terms of realistic, practical facts (S) or trends, patterns and future forecasts (N). When this function is exaggerated during stress it leads to procrastination as no amount of data will be sufficient for you to feel comfortable making a decision.

Alternatively, if your dominant function is Thinking (ESTJ, ENTJ, ISTP, INTP) or Feeling (ESFJ, ENFJ, ISFP, INFP), then in stressful situations you are likely to close down your options too early by using too much logical critique (T) or values and ethics (F). When this function is exaggerated during stress you will find yourself making rash decisions without sufficient information and you will become blinkered and stubborn. Furthermore, if your dominant function is Extraverted, you will spend more and more time externalising through brainstorming or checking facts out with others, becoming shallow and reactive, and spend less and less time reflecting and thinking through what your decisions could be. If, instead, your dominant function is Introverted then you will spend more and more time alone sifting through the available information, becoming withdrawn and uncommunicative, and spend less and less time being attentive to what is going on around you or checking with others.

All this sounds like very bad news but, once again, Type can come to the rescue by suggesting that you rely on your second strongest tent peg – your auxiliary function. For all Types, your auxiliary function is attempting to do the opposite to your dominant function. If your dominant function is involved in 'divergent thinking' by constantly gathering information (dominant S or N), then your auxiliary function is your favourite way to make decisions (auxiliary T or F) by pruning the options and giving you a clearer way forward. If your dominant function is involved in 'convergent thinking' by making swift decisions (dominant T or F) then your auxiliary function is your favourite way to inform those decisions by providing relevant data (auxiliary S or N).

So if you can work out your auxiliary function, you have a ready-made stress management tool personalised for your type! In the above examples, my ESTJ sister could have engaged her auxiliary function (Introverted Sensing) and utilised the information that, in the past, I have chosen to drive up to her house on the Saturday morning and not the night before as I am tired from my working week and want to relax on the Friday evening instead of making the long drive then. (I have usually neglected to pack in time as well!) So she could use this information for her 'Plan A' and then, using Introverted Sensing, come up with one or two realistic contingency plans (e.g. shopping on Saturday morning OR afternoon and planning options for meals depending on the time available to cook ('Plan Z' being the local chippy).

Allan's auxiliary function is extraverted Thinking, so he might have been more effective by applying some structure, like a spreadsheet, and only looking at amounts above £50 as (logically) these were the most important items to factor into a household budget. A logical framework could then have been implemented and shared with the family.

## Stress management tips for all Types

So what are the hints and tips that your auxiliary function might suggest to distress your life?

### Introverted Types

Generally speaking, Introverts will withdraw when they are stressed, so engaging their auxiliary function will help to bring them back into the real world.

**If you are an ISTJ or ISFJ,** then in stressful situations you may find yourself becoming quietly obsessed with the accuracy of information. You might become nit picky or convinced that data has to be verified again and again. To de-stress, ISTJs will need to engage extraverted Thinking – putting all the gathered data into some logical order and cutting down the options using cause and effect thinking. However, ISFJs, will instead need to look to extraverted Feeling for help. Sharing problems (and the data) with close friends works well for ISFJs as getting some advice from someone who cares will enable them to make decisions and stop procrastinating.

**INFJs and INTJs** get overwhelmed with possibilities when under stress. Catastrophising every eventuality will get them falling down the introverted iNtuition rabbit hole (how apt to use a metaphor!) For INFJs it's extraverted Feeling that can save them. For them, a problem shared is a problem halved (close friends work better for Introverts). INTJs will be better off extraverting their ideas into a mind-map, and start engaging extraverted Thinking to critique it and decide which ideas to prune. Using the right technique allows each introverted iNtuitive to stop procrastinating and make some badly-needed decisions to move forwards.

**ISTPs and INTPs** can get very self-critical during stress. They apply their ability to spot flaws in their own performance, which can cripple them. Using extraverted Sensing helps to de-stress ISTPs. This might involve taking a walk outside (preferably with friends), working out at the gym watching the TV monitors or playing some team sport, like football. Practising mindfulness is an excellent way to de-stress and taps heavily into extraverted Sensing, so ISTPs (although initially cynical) might benefit more than other Types from this form of meditation to bring people into the 'here and now'. INTPs, on the other hand, would benefit from engaging their extraverted iNtuition to brainstorm (with others) possible ways out of the stressful situation and adopting a more optimistic 'can do' attitude.

**ISFPs and INFPs** can feel like the world is against them when they experience stress. An overwhelming feeling of incongruence is very unsettling to these Types if they find themselves in a situation they feel is unethical or unreasonably cold and impersonal. INFPs can turn to their most trusted friends for a brainstorm of options to get themselves out of the situation. This will engage their extraverted iNtuition and free up their options enabling them to see a way out. ISFPs would do better engaging extraverted Sensing instead. Mindfulness would be a great option for ISFPs who can get in touch with what's really happening by just 'being' in the moment and not using their dominant function to push for hasty decisions. Like ISTPs, team sports or lively activities can also help ISFPs de-stress.

### Extraverted Types

Extraverts will tend to become more outgoing in their attempt to deal with stressful situations. What they really need to do to get the balance back in their lives is to remove themselves from the source of stress and spend some time reflecting with their introverted auxiliary function.

**ESTPs and ESFPs** become more and more risky in their behaviour as they become stressed. Some will even over-indulge their senses by overeating, drinking or other interesting sensual experiences (I will leave these to your imagination!). ESTPs can refocus by reflecting on the logical decisions that have to be made and using cause and effect thinking to quietly analyse what is the root of the stress and how to eliminate it. ESFPs can de-stress by getting in touch with their deeply held values and beliefs. Deciding how they can act authentically to these values in the stressful situation will free them from becoming locked in the present and allow them to move forwards to the future.

**ENFPs and ENTPs** love variety but under stress they can take this too far and become overwhelmed by possibilities. They can generate far more ideas than can ever be implemented and feel unable to choose which ones might work best. What they need to do is to spend some time alone, quietly weighing up their options and rejecting the less practical ones. ENTPs will use cause and effect thinking and logic to make these critical decisions, while ENFPs will be using values and considering what is best for the people involved. In these stressful situations, the ability to make good decisions is better than generating endless theoretical options.

**ESTJs and ENTJs** will try hard to control stressful situations by imposing structure and order into their lives. ESTJs can alleviate their stress by spending time alone writing detailed lists of practical things to do to fix the crisis. Gathering relevant facts about the situation will also help to inform their dominant Thinking process with realistic information. This will help to 'ground' them instead of making uninformed, rash decisions. ENTJs, on the other hand, will benefit from time alone to shift their thinking (even paradigm shifting if that is possible) to view the stressful situation in a new light. New options can free them from feeling trapped and believing that there is no way out. Envisioning a different brighter future can help to bring them back on track.

**ESFJs and ENFJs** become unnaturally bossy when stressed. Extraverted Feeling may be a function searching for harmony, but it's still a Judging function and other people still feel pushed around if it's unnecessarily exaggerated. ESFJs need to spend time alone checking the reality of the situation using their introverted Sensing and recalling experiences from the past of what has helped or hindered them in previous similar situations. ENFJs are more likely to de-stress by finding somewhere quiet, away from others and envisioning an outcome to the stressful situation where everyone is better off. Using introverted iNtuition to imagine this harmonious future state will give them the vision to work through the stressful situation.

So we can see that Personality Type has the power to predict what each of us will find stressful, and how we will react. It also has some useful answers for us by letting us know what activities each Type can use to manage the stress and get back in balance. To quote Andrew Bernstein (who has had the benefit of lecturing in philosophy at both Harvard and Yale): "The truth is that stress doesn't come from your boss, your kids, your spouse, traffic jams, health challenges, or other circumstances. It comes from your thoughts about these circumstances." If this is true then we already have the tools to manage stress and Type has the power to unleash it.

# Angelina Bennet

Angelina runs iPotential consulting, who specialise in team development and coaching. She is also the president of the British Association of Psychological Type, so we know that we're in the presence of a serious expert. Mind you, serious is not a word I'd usually use to describe Angelina's work. Yes, she is deeply knowledgeable and hugely clever, to the extent that she is respected by other Type experts and gurus. What sets Angelina aside is that she carries this expertise with a humble nature and self-effacing humour that makes it so easy for her clients to take on board her thoughts and suggestions.

Angelina is a strong proponent of looking at Type as a whole – she would remind you to look beyond the four individual letters of your Type to understand what the whole says about you. With that in mind, in this chapter she is exploring a fascinating issue – how different levels of personal development relate to each of the Personality Types.

Gareth

# :: Type & Ego Development – From 1D to 3D Coaching

By Angelina Bennet

## From observation to question

I have been working with Personality Type for around 15 years in a variety of ways. I nearly always use Type when I am coaching individuals and teams, and, as a qualifying trainer, I have trained up a good few hundred practitioners and observed a good few hundred feedbacks. I also attend conferences worldwide held by Type associations, such as the British Association for Psychological Type (BAPT), Association of Type International (APTi) and the European Association for Psychological Type (EAPT). All of this has given me exposure to a huge variety of individuals who have had their Type identified. Sadly, I am much more likely to remember the Type of someone I have met than I am to remember their name.

From all this exposure to people of different Types, I started to notice differences between people of the same Types. Of course we are all individuals with our own characteristics, experiences, world view, etc., and Type mainly describes commonalities in drives and motivations rather than behaviour or character itself. In fact, one of my favourite Type quotes comes from Mary McCaulley, and states:

*"Each person is unique. An ENFP is like every other ENFP, like some other ENFPs, and like no other ENFP." (McCaulley, 2000)*

However, aside from individual characteristics, I observed differences in the effectiveness with which people expressed their Type. I noticed that some people may be restricted or limited by their Type, refusing to get out of their comfort zone, while others of the same Type may appear more flexible and adaptable. Likewise, for some people, the

139

negative aspects of their Type were in evidence more often than the positive qualities. For example, the differences between two ENTPs on a Type workshop – one kept interrupting (derailing the flow of the course) with suggestions on how the course could be better designed, while the other interjected at appropriate times with ideas and questions about the possible applications of Type. This made me question whether there was a specific individual difference that influenced personal effectiveness. The difference seemed to be about more than emotional intelligence, more than cognitive intelligence, more than self-awareness, and more than maturity. So what exactly was this difference? One single variable, or a combination of factors?

At the time, I knew very little about Type development theory. The Type training described how the order of functions may emerge during one's lifetime, and how the non-preferred aspects could start to appear after midlife, but this did not seem to say anything about individual effectiveness. Jung had more to say about Type development, but I did not become aware of this until later, and even then it did not really answer my question.

### From questions to possible answers

It was around this time, and quite by chance, that I found out about the Enneagram, which is another personality Type system, similar in some ways to the Myers-Briggs model but very different in other ways. There are several different Enneagram theorists who all have a slightly different view on it, but I attended the training course by Don Riso and Russ Hudson. Their approach was unique from the others because, on top of the descriptions of the Types, they had added different levels of functioning which they described as Healthy Levels, Average Levels and Unhealthy Levels. Therefore, each Type could be described in terms of what they would look like if they were well functioning right through to how they may experience mental health problems.

This insight could not have come at a better time for me. This was exactly what I thought the Myers-Briggs approach was missing! So I set about looking for ways to describe each Type at its best, as it is typically expressed, and at its most dysfunctional, but without going as far as actual mental health issues.

At first all I had were single word descriptors for each Type spread across five levels, which were called: (1) Adaptable & Effective, (2) Flexible & Well-balanced, (3) Typical, (4) Entrenched & Lacking Balance and (5) Defensive & Ineffective. I also started to consider where Type was placed within the wider context of the psyche, and, although that is another story, some aspects of this work came into the exploration of Type effectiveness. With all this work and research going on, I made the (in retrospect, terrible) decision to turn this into a doctoral thesis. (To cut to the chase, it all worked out in the end, but it was not a pleasant journey.) I was not allowed to make up my own levels of effectiveness to combine with Type, but had to find an established and existing theory to base it on. Luckily, I stumbled upon a theory that completely fitted with my thinking and was already well developed.

## From Opportunist to Magician

The theory that I came across was Ego Development Theory by Susanne Cook-Greuter (2004), which in itself was a further development of the original theory by Jane Loevinger (1976). This theory suggests that most individuals go through several distinct stages of development from birth to adulthood.

I will describe the stages in more detail later, but broadly speaking, at each stage there is an increase in self-awareness, a better understanding of others, a broadening of perspective, less defensiveness, increased mindfulness, increased spiritual awareness, plus several more aspects. When a person is functioning at a particular stage of development, it can be difficult for them to see beyond that stage, yet they can look back on themselves at earlier stages and see how they may have had a limited perspective. Consider for a moment ... do you remember, probably in your teens, being convinced that you knew pretty much all there was to know about life, and certainly as much as your parents knew? (If you answered 'no' to that question, you must have been a uniquely lovely teenager!) And now, looking back, you realise that you knew nothing then and probably still know nothing now?

## The forest analogy

If a person were to live deep in the forest and never emerge from it, their reality would consist of trees, plants, a few animals, etc. They would have no idea that anything else could possibly exist, other than their own reality. Supposing one day, they climb to the top of the tallest tree in the forest and catch sight of a snow-capped mountain in the distance. Suddenly their existing concept of the world being made up of trees, plants, etc. is no longer true. With some trepidation they may leave the forest and travel towards the mountain, learning about the new terrain as they go. From here they can look back on the forest and see that it is only a part of the entire landscape after all and realise that their previous perspective was somewhat narrow and basic. At some point they may decide to climb the mountain and, at the summit, they look out in a new direction and catch sight of the ocean. Once again, their existing reality no longer explains everything. Their journey may take them on to deserts, jungles, cities, polar caps ... With every step, their perception of the world is broadened, they can cope with more complexity and, eventually they will realise that the world is one inter-dependent eco-system.

Development from one level to another can occur naturally with age, as more complex situations and relationships become part of life, as a result of challenging experiences, or following deliberate personal development (e.g. coaching or therapy). There are a couple of things to note, however:

- With this model, the most important thing is to be functioning at a level of development that is appropriate to your life situation. It is not about trying to get to the top.
- People do not consistently function at their maximum level of development, but may fluctuate through several levels in a day.
- Pressure and stress may cause us to revert to earlier levels of development.
- Transition from one stage to another can often be accompanied by a period of personal disturbance and confusion.
- Different aspects of ourselves may develop at different times. So, for example, a person may be at a more advanced stage of development in terms of having a broad perspective cognitively, but may be at an earlier stage of development with regard to their self-awareness.
- Anxiety and depression (Neuroticism, to give it its technical name) can exist at any stage of development.
- People can function well at any stage apart from the Power and Control stage where relationships may be difficult.

So, before we look at the levels in more detail, there is one more thing to note. Both Loevinger's and Cook-Greuter's names for the levels were not 'Type neutral', in that some of the labels sounded like some of the names often given to certain Types. Therefore, I have renamed the stages to be Type neutral and also to better suit their application to Type theory. Additionally, I only use seven out of Cook-Greuter's nine levels.

The following is a brief summary of the main features of each level. I have put Cook-Greuter's original names in parentheses next to the names that I came up with.

### Level of Power and Control (Opportunist)

Individuals at this level are largely ineffective and are likely to have relationship difficulties. They are operating from the point of view of survival of the fittest and see every situation or interaction as something they need to win. They have little to no awareness of the needs or motives of others and will not understand compromise or consultation. Few adults will function mainly out of this level unless they have had issues during their upbringing. This is a stage often seen in very young children, for example, caught red-handed yet denying all and/or blaming someone else.

### Level of Social Identification (Diplomat)

Individuals who function at this level may have fairly smooth social relationships with the people and groups that they choose to associate with. However, they may not be in touch with their real selves and will be intolerant of those who are different. The primary concern is being seen to fit in. This is often evident in teenagers who may express their group identity via fashion and music. Unfortunately, adults can revert to this stage fairly easily when in groups. For example, when you see us vs. them behaviour in workplaces – Sales vs. Marketing, Accounts vs. HR, and Everyone vs. IT!

### Level of Personal Identity (Expert)

Individuals who function at this level have some idea of what they are actually like as a person and attempt to find their niche or cultivate relationships that are more in tune with who they are. Generally, they can function fairly well at this stage when working in their comfort zone. However, they will have difficulty with difference. This stage is fine for the technical expert roles where there is little need for people management.

### Level of Determined Action (Achiever)

Individuals operating at this level are concerned with achieving goals and maximising personal strengths. They are likely to have a good sense of who they are and how they differ from others, and will have some appreciation of the value of these differences.

### *Level of Considerate Individualism (Individualist)*

Individuals who function at this level have a very good sense of self-awareness and a genuine appreciation for the differences in others. They are able to take multiple perspectives on matters and recognise there is not always one clear answer or way. However, this ability to see many sides can cause inner confusion.

### *Level of Integration and Authenticity (Strategist)*

Individuals at this level demonstrate authenticity and will respond to challenge without defensiveness. They have the ability to see everything as part of a wider system and can adapt and respond appropriately to complex situations.

### *Magician Level (Magician)*

This rare level of insight enables individuals to take multiple perspectives on complex issues and generate seemingly impossible solutions. Individuals at this level have incredible self-awareness and often operate in a state of 'flow'.

(As this book is about Personality Type, from this point on I will only use my Type-neutral names for the developmental levels.)

Most adults tend to plateau their development at the Personal Identity or Determined Action levels. Although most people can function fairly well at all levels except for the Power & Control Level, as previously mentioned, it is important that the level of development matches the individual's role in life. Therefore, it is generally accepted that a good people manager should really have the capacity for the Determined Action Level, whereas those in positions of considerable leadership will be effective at the Considerate Individualism Level. Very few individuals reach the later stages of development.

## Case Study – Brian

Brian's employer was offering their staff the opportunity to have a coaching session using MBTI. Brian showed an interest and met me for the session. I asked what he knew about Personality Type and why he thought it may be useful for him at this point. He explained that he'd heard it could be useful for working with others. He told me that he had been under pressure recently and that he didn't feel as if he was at his best. Others were telling him that he was coming across as fairly blunt, critical and impatient. Brian added that sometimes he would offend people without realising why.

Our Type discussion indicated that Brian was probably an extraverted Thinking Type (ENTJ), but was, at that time, using Thinking in a very one-sided manner and often showing the rough side of the Thinking preference. This is fairly characteristic of people at the Personal Identity stage. However, the fact that Brian had requested the coaching and had explained that he was under pressure and that things were not going as well as usual, indicated that he may usually operate at the Determined Action stage. A further indication of this was that he was taking action to do something about it and wanted to get a clear outcome from the session.

So the work focused on helping Brian identify his 'default settings' and Type, and exploring what he could identify in people of the opposite Types. As the session was a comfortable environment, Brian was able to be more relaxed and appeared to be operating at the Determined Action level. We explored the sources of the stress, and what situations enabled Brian to be at his best. Between us we created a clear action plan to help him to restore the balance in himself.

## From horizontal to vertical

Ego development theory is sometimes referred to as a 'vertical' theory of development because of its sequential nature, whilst development that is concerned with increasing an individual's current awareness through information may be referred to as 'horizontal' development. The standard use of the Myers-Briggs would fall into the category of horizontal development as the focus is on raising awareness, exploring what is typical, and exploring how somebody experiences their Type and the differences between themselves and others. From part of my doctoral research I discovered that development actions that follow a Myers-Briggs session are usually confined to considering how the individual may use their non-preferred styles and flex their style to accommodate others.

Both Cook-Greuter and Ken Wilber note that the absence of a vertical dimension is a significant limitation of typologies, such as the Myers-Briggs. In Cook-Greuter's work, she notes that the current Myers-Briggs model comes under the heading of "Different, but equal", in that all Types are equally valid and what matters is the fit between an individual's style and the context in which they are operating. She suggests that, *"... another way people differ from each other, the developmental stage, is as important and sometimes more so than how they differ in personality Type and preferences"* (2004, p.276).

I have to say that since I have been using both models together, I agree with her statement. In some situations the difference between Types seems to be the root cause of an issue, and in other situations the mismatch between developmental stage and role or relationship can be the issue. However, it follows that if an individual of a given Type is operating at an early stage of development, he or she may not be able to adapt and flex their style to meet Type-challenging situations, whereas an individual at a higher level of development will be more able to adapt his or her behaviour to suit different situations. Therefore, combining the developmental stage with psychological Type can add a whole new dimension to understanding individuals, how their Types may be expressed and what their further development needs may be. In fact, rather than being a 2 dimensional model (horizontal x vertical), I actually see it as 3 dimensional because it allows you to also include depth. Considering where an individual is regarding their developmental stage gives an indication of the level of depth that you can work with (knowledge, experience and qualifications permitting). More about this in the applications section.

## From Two Separate Theories to One Unified Theory

For each of the 16 Types, I combined Type Theory with Ego Development Theory to come up with a description of each Type at seven levels of development. These descriptions were originally based on theory and observation, then checked with several individuals of each Type to get their comments and any amendments. I still consider it to be somewhat a work in progress as I have ideas on how I want to develop this further. Nevertheless, many of the Type practitioners who have read my work tell me that the descriptions have been insightful for both themselves and their clients.

The table below outlines an abbreviated example of the ENTP seven stage description.

| Ego Development Stage | Example of Developmentally Levelled Type Description (ENTP) |
|---|---|
| **Level of power & control** *Individuals at this level are largely ineffective and are likely to have disrupted or dysfunctional relationships. They are operating from the point of view of survival of the fittest and see every situation or interaction as something they need to win. They have little to no awareness of the needs or motives of others and will not understand compromise or consultation.* | At this level, ENTPs are likely to react to most situations using a distortion of their dominant extraverted iNtuition preference and will often be seen as brash, rebellious, hasty and novelty-seeking. They will use their auxiliary introverted Thinking to look for flaws and imperfections, however, this can lead to blunt and often inappropriately positioned suggestions as to how things should be changed to make them better. As extraverted Types, they will argue and challenge relentlessly in an attempt to shout down those who they are in conflict with and can appear confrontational, unwilling to listen, abrasive and condescending. ENTPs enjoy challenging the status quo and playing devil's advocate, however, when operating at this level, they a can become relentlessly adversarial and unwilling to drop an argument, often using distorted logic to try and push their viewpoint. |

| | |
|---|---|
| *Level of social identification*<br><br>*Individuals who function at this level may have fairly smooth social relationships with the people and groups they choose to associate with, however, they may not be in touch with their real selves and will be intolerant of those who are different. Their primary concern is being seen to fit in.* | Whether ENTPs find themselves in Type-supportive or non-supportive groups, they will often try to get into a position of influence within the group but not necessarily want to be in the main leadership position. If they are not the group leader, they are likely to only want to follow a leader they look up to and respect. They will often take the role of leading others in the group to have fun or even get up to mischief. Often, ENTPs consider their 'group' as being superior to others. If their ENTP characteristics do not 'fit' they may suppress their natural styles and make clumsy use of their under-developed non-preferred functions. |
| *Level of personal identity*<br><br>*Individuals who function at this level have some idea of what they are actually like as a person and attempt to find their niche or cultivate relationships that are more in tune with who they are. Generally they can function fairly well at this stage when working in their comfort zone, however, they will have difficulty with difference.* | ENTPs at this level begin to channel their dominant extraverted iNtuition into their lives and work; looking for new initiatives, generating new ideas, scanning the environment for inspiration and seeking improvements in an energetic and often light hearted/humorous manner. Whatever they do, they will want to be seen as original and innovative and can be fairly competitive with others in this arena. They will prefer to work in environments that allow a high degree of independence and will often look for positions that challenge their intellect. However they may push their Type preferences too strongly at times and become novelty-seeking, easily bored, opinionated, impatient, uninhibited, abrupt and impulsive. |

| *Level of determined action* | ENTPs at this level really begin to use the |
|---|---|
| *Individuals operating at this level are concerned with achieving goals and maximising personal strengths. They are likely to have a good sense of who they are and how they differ from others, and will have some appreciation of the value of these differences.* | ENTPs at this level really begin to use the strengths of their preferences and will be versatile, questioning, energetic, rational, objective and curious. They will be change oriented, aware of future possibilities, analytical and comfortable with taking appropriate risks. They will realise that they have some blind spots, and they are likely to begin to realise that there is some value to be gained from S and F ways. Therefore, they may seek viewpoints from those they see as different to themselves, however, they will only incorporate these ideas if they do not go against their own preferences too strongly. |
| *Level of considerate individualism* | ENTPs will move away from using the |
| *Individuals who function at this level have a very good sense of self-awareness and a genuine appreciation for the differences in others. They are able to take multiple perspectives on matters and recognise there is not always one clear answer or way.* | ENTPs will move away from using the strengths of their Type to look for new or different ideas, and move towards using these strengths to be innovative, creative and entrepreneurial. They will be conceptual and strategic, making good use of their auxiliary introverted Thinking and critically evaluating their ideas. They will be constructively challenging rather than just being critical, and they will seek opportunities rather than novelty. They no longer thrive on recognition for their originality and spontaneity, and are likely to feel more content with 'what is' instead of constantly seeking 'what could be'. |

| | |
|---|---|
| **Level of Integration &** **Authenticity** *Individuals at this level demonstrate authenticity and will respond to challenge without defensiveness. They have the ability to see everything as part of a wider system and can adapt and respond appropriately to complex situations.* | The qualities of the ENTP preferences can shine through – they will be seen as innovative, resourceful, imaginative, enterprising, ingenious, adaptable and insightful. The ENTP can appear to be a visionary thinker, seeing patterns that may not be obvious to others, creating global solutions and being quick to respond to changes in the environment. They are no longer concerned with defending their image of originality and independence and enjoy the learning they get from being with a variety of other people. Through increased mindfulness, they will often be able to access their S and F preferences. |
| **Magician level** *This rare level of insight enables individuals to take multiple perspectives on complex issues and generate seemingly impossible solutions. Individuals at this level have incredible self-awareness and operate in a state of 'flow'.* | The ENTP realises that their drive for originality, innovation and improvement is ego driven and a distraction from their true self. They will also be more accepting of others being who they are, realising that encouraging others to develop and be original is also a function of their own ego. Being able to let go of dualities, they will see that Feeling is part of the same concept as Thinking, and that Sensing is part of the same concept as iNtuition, seeing the similarities in the functions rather than the differences and therefore being able to gain easy and natural access to S and F. At this stage, they may also frequently experience the Transcendent function – where from two apparent opposites a third way emerges, often in a form that is symbolic or intuitive. |

Fuller descriptions for each of the 16 Types can be found in my book, *The Shadows of Type: Psychological Type through Seven Levels of Development.*

Perhaps you can refer back to my example of the two different ENTPs on the training course and take a guess which levels they were each operating from?

### Case study – Janice

Janice worked in a public service department that was undergoing significant change. She had been tasked with carrying this change process through. Her Type had already been identified in an earlier team session as ISTJ. Janice had been provided with a series of coaching sessions to help support her in her work with the change process. On the one hand, she didn't think this was a good use of time, but also liked having the opportunity to voice her frustrations with some of the people in her team.

Janice made comments such as, "I see that some of them are worried, but we've got a job to get on with so there's no point in moaning about it", and "We've had so many meetings now, and I just say my piece and then sit back again. Every meeting I say the same thing. I've even started beginning with "Now this is the last time I'm going to say this …" From these statements, it seemed apparent that Janice had very little understanding of people who had different reactions to her, and very little awareness of the impact of her style on others. There was evidence of fairly black and white thinking, and of a mind already made up that would not be changed. This seemed to be evidence of the Personal Identity stage being most prevalent.

## From theory to application

Some of the applications of this horizontal + vertical approach to using Type are:

- Giving feedback – how deep can you go?
- Coaching – how might the individual react to the coaching?
- Setting development goals – what is the next appropriate step for them?
- Personal development – how balanced is he/she likely to be in using their Type?
- Conflict – what happens to the Type when they become defensive?
- Stress & pressure – how might the Type look when the person is under pressure?
- Leadership – what stage is the individual currently functioning in and what do they need to do to function at an appropriate level for leadership?
- Succession planning – what does the individual need to develop in order to progress?

For this chapter I will focus on the first two applications – Giving feedback and Coaching.

## Giving feedback & Coaching

Since working in this way I have been able to tailor my Myers-Briggs feedback sessions more appropriately to the individual. I can use my estimation of the client's developmental stage to anticipate how they may approach the session, and this can help me to build rapport and tailor my style to suit. I can also use this information to assess how far to go with the Type work.

The table below summarises how individuals at different developmental stages may approach the work and at what depth you might be able to work with them appropriate to their developmental level.

| Power & Control | Anyone who is functioning at this level or who has reverted to this level due to stress or defensiveness is likely to be hostile towards the idea of coaching and see it as a battle of wills. They will demonstrate black and white thinking and have little capacity for objective self-reflection. Usually they are unaware that there is any other valid way of operating than their own. If you are working with Type with individuals at this stage, it may be enough for them just to find out that not everybody thinks and sees the world as they do. Don't expect them to show much appreciation for people who are opposite to them. |
|---|---|
| Social Identification | People functioning at this level are likely to play a 'role' in coaching or therapy (e.g. ideal client). You may observe lots of conflict between self and 'should-be' self. They are likely to be aware that there are different groups of people, and some groups are 'better' than others. They may use a lot of 'shoulds', 'musts' and 'oughts' during the session, and be focused on what they think they should be like. Type work could focus on the message that all Types are valuable and attempt to get them to recognise their best fit. |
| Personal Identity | These individuals may have come with a preconceived idea of what Type is about. Therefore, the coach may need to spend some time undoing some of these preconceptions. The client may not see any need for personal development, or they may consider you to be the expert and expect you to tell them what they need to do. They are likely to have some awareness of different/opposite styles, but little appreciation for opposites. Type work could focus on how appropriate their style is in a variety of situations, and asking them if they feel that they would benefit in some situations by a different approach? Also, start to promote some appreciation of the opposites. |
| Integration & Authenticity | At this stage the inner conflicts are likely to be more resolved. Coaching sessions may be used mainly as an opportunity for reflection. Individuals at this level may be able to access the real energy of the opposite preference (as opposed to a surface behaviour) and use it appropriately. Type may be very flexible at this stage and present fewer challenges. The client is likely to set the agenda for the sessions. |

| Determined Action | At this stage, individuals are likely to engage well and take responsibility during coaching. They may have even requested coaching, but may take a 'task' approach – "what do I need to do?" They will see progress by goal achievement. They are likely to be aware of difference/ opposites and have some appreciation for how diversity can add value.<br><br>Type work at this level could start to explore variations in their own expression and use of Type. What brings out the best in them? What brings out the worst in them? And how easy is it for them to flex their style and remain authentic? Concluding with some sort of action plan will fit well with their expectations. |
|---|---|
| Considerate Individualism | At this level, individuals are likely to have a good capacity for self-reflection and seeing multiple aspects, but may feel conflicted because of this. They are likely to see the connections and contexts of issues. They'll probably value the time and space for reflection and use the coaching sessions for this. One common issue is that they are likely to experience tension and inner conflict between the opposites within themselves.<br><br>Type work could explore these opposites, explore the balance within their Type, explore their shadow sides, and discuss their interactions with others. |
| Magician | Here, opposites can work together in synergy. At this stage, individuals may frequently experience the 'transcendent function'.<br><br>Their approach to the sessions and the coach's role is likely to be similar to the previous stage. |

**Case study – Paul**

Paul had been familiar with Type for quite a while, as he had gone through the process at work, and later done some additional self-study. His preferences were for INTP and my estimate of his developmental stage was Considerate Individualist. He was in a leadership position and had requested coaching every two months to support him in his role. During our coaching sessions, Paul demonstrated a good level of self-awareness, a good insight into the motivations of others, and a real willingness to keep learning and developing. He seemed to be able to genuinely see things from other people's point of view. The main issue that Paul was having was that people would get frustrated with himself for changing and adapting plans. He explained that he could often see so many different viewpoints, and then new information would often come in, and this would alter his perspective again.

Paul tended to use the coaching sessions for time and space to reflect and explore, rather than to develop any clear action plans. He very much guided the sessions himself. Type was often referred to. Although Paul demonstrated a lot of adaptability and flexibility in how he used his Type, Type was still working away in the background. He seemed to use the gifts of his Type very effectively and often manage to catch himself before falling into the common traps for INTPs.

## From measurement to instinct

I am frequently asked (and I expect you are thinking it too) how to assess an individual's developmental level. Loevinger originally came up with a tool called the Sentence Completion Test for use in her research, where the individual is asked to complete a sentence in any way the like. For example, "Rules are ..." or "A husband has the right to ...". Cook-Greuter and colleagues used a similar sentence completion approach to create the Leadership Development Profile (Harthill

Consulting). However, these assessments are difficult to interpret and to score, and also one must question how they will then use the information provided.

Asking an individual to estimate their level of development is also problematic. Those at the Personal Identity level often rate themselves as Magicians. This is because a feature of that level is to think that you know pretty much everything. Those who are at the later stages of development often rate themselves as being at earlier stages, because a feature of the later stages is to realise how much is still unknown.

In the table below, Cook-Greuter provides a summary of various studies that she has carried out regarding the distribution of the developmental level in the general adult population assessed using the Leadership Development Profile. From this data it would seem that the *Expert* (Personal Identity) level of development is where most people operate from, followed by the *Achiever* (Determined Action) level.

| Developmental Level | 535 managers and consultants in the UK | 497 managers and supervisors in the USA | 4510 USA mixed adult population |
|---|---|---|---|
| *Ironist* | 0.9 | <1 | 0.5 |
| *Magician* | 5.6 | <1 | 1.5 |
| *Strategist* | 13.5 | 1.4 | 4.9 |
| *Individualist* | 23.4 | 5 | 11.3 |
| *Achiever* | 33.5 | 34.8 | 29.7 |
| *Expert* | 21.1 | 47.8 | 36.5 |
| *Diplomat* | 1.7 | 8.2 | 11.3 |
| *Impulsive and Opportunist* | 0.4 | 2.2 | 4.3 |

*Distribution of the levels of development (%)*

Cook-Greuter notes that the difference in the UK distribution compared with the USA distribution is thought to be a result of the sample being volunteers for the study, and that those who are at later stages are more likely to volunteer for such research.

I usually find that a short way into a conversation, particularly about Type, I can get a broad brush idea of where an individual tends to be regarding their developmental level. Bearing in mind that most people are likely to be at the Personal Identity or Determined Action stages, I tend to look for any evidence that they may be at a different stage and, if there is nothing to suggest this, then try to estimate which of these 'average' levels they may be functioning at. Their approach to the sessions and their current levels of self-awareness as described in the table on the earlier page can be an indication.

Sometimes I ask a specific question, such as "How would you define leadership?" or "Have you ever changed anything about yourself in response to feedback?" I often find that the way in which these questions are answered can provide some clues. Those at earlier stages tend to define leadership in terms of the control of others, or in a command and control style. The Personal Identity stage tend to attach some sort of qualifying knowledge or expertise to the leadership role, where those at the Determined Action may start to talk more about guiding, empowering, and co-ordinating others. At the later stages there may be mention of leaders being in supportive or facilitating roles, or even mention of ideas, such as servant-leadership.

Regarding the changes in response to feedback, often those at the earlier stages struggle with the idea of feedback, or see feedback as criticism. They are likely to describe how they didn't change. At the later stages it is likely that the individual will be able to reflect on this question well, provide examples, and show that they really valued the feedback given. Again, it is difficult to be absolutely precise, but the more you explore the question the more will come out.

### Developing yourself

Moving from one stage to another is not an easy process, nor one that can be prescribed. Most people develop due to mind-broadening experiences, things that take them out of their comfort zone, overcoming challenges, and taking the time to reflect on these experiences. The transition between stages can also be a bumpy path, characterised by disruption, turmoil, regression to earlier behaviours, anxiety, etc., as our world view shatters and a new world view starts to come into focus.

Some things you can do to develop yourself are:

- Travel to different places and explore new cultural perspectives.
- Get into work or other groups with people who are different to you.
- Create an aspirational career development plan and consider what you would need to develop to get there.
- Look at ways to enhance your self-awareness and awareness of others, such as Type work. Don't just stop exploring once you know your best fit!
- Take time to reflect on and/or to discuss personal development with others.
- Learn from failure and difficult circumstances.

And remember, development is not about trying to get to the 'top', but it is about ensuring that your outlook on life is congruent with your life circumstances.

## From question to conclusion

The combination of Ego Development Theory with Type Theory has helped to answer the question I had about effectiveness of Type. It may add more complexity to working with Type, but it is important to note that Type is not a simple concept. The beauty of Type is that a practitioner can choose to use it in a variety of ways to suit the situation, from simple and basic, to complex and deep. However, the more knowledge of the complexity and depth that a practitioner has, the more tailored and effective their Type work can be. Ego Development Theory is only one of many theories that complement Psychological Type. I would strongly urge any Type practitioner to continue their learning about Type and related theories, and also to continue to reflect on their own Type development.

I think I learn something new about Type at least once a week. It could just be a new perspective, a real-life example of Type at work, or the result of training or conference attendance. For me, Type is a concept that continues to unfold. It really does require life-long learning. So, in conclusion, there isn't really a conclusion ... more questions will follow, more ideas will emerge, more exploration will take place. Well, at least that's how Type is for me.

## References

Bennet, A. (2010) *The Shadows of Type: Psychological Type through Seven Levels of Development.* Lulu

Cook-Greuter, S. (2004) *Making the Case for a Developmental Perspective. Industrial and Commercial Training* 36(7): 275-281.

Loevinger, J. (1976) *Ego development.* London, Jossey-Bass Publishers.

McCaulley, M. in Briggs-Myers, I. (2000) *Introduction to Type.* CPP, Inc.

Riso, D. & Hudson, R. (1996) *Personality Types: Using the Enneagram for Self-Discovery.* (Revised) New York, Houghton Mifflin.

Wilber, K. (2000) *Integral Psychology.* Boston, Shambhala.

# Bernard Cooke

I've known Bernard for many years and we've worked together on many projects. I've always found that his wry intelligence helps to get his message across. He's certainly used it many times to help me confront my own truths that I'd been ignoring.

Bernard is best known as a coach and for his work on leadership development workshops. He has been running Cookes Consulting for eight years, during which time he has helped hundreds of people to learn more about themselves and to improve their performance. As such a well-respected coach and consultant, we should consider ourselves fortunate therefore that he has been willing to take the time to share some of his experiences in this book.

Bernard's chapter is about taking risks in coaching, so he might have worried that he was putting his own reputation on the line. Well, the reputation remains firmly in place throughout the following pages, even if his trousers don't.

Gareth

# :: Type Theory and Leadership – The dark and light side of coaching

By Bernard Cooke

## Introduction

OK, I admit it – I have a morbid fascination and gain genuine enjoyment out of looking at the dark side of things. I may be considered very old fashioned and outdated by fellow coaching psychologists who tell me that focusing on dysfunction and figuring out why things go wrong and how to fix them is just not the way that we should operate these days. Instead, we should be embracing the principles of positive psychology and encouraging our clients to realise their strengths and apply themselves to achieving well-being and success. But if you call me a pessimistic 'glass half empty' person rather than a 'glass half full' optimist, then I would say that you've got me wrong, because I think we can see both! All I'm suggesting is that if we are interested in the contents of the glass (to continue the metaphor) then we should understand the nature of both the fullness and the emptiness. And if we want to facilitate some change in the contents of our glass, then we had better understand something about what makes it full and what makes it empty! Personally, I have gained invaluable insights from Type theory, including why I sometimes struggle to be the best that I can be and why my behaviour can transform into something rather weird and dysfunctional. In my coaching and training work I encourage people to look at themselves in totality, to learn what both the bright and dark sides have to offer. And in pioneering spirit I have confronted my own dark side by dropping my trousers in front of a group of prestigious executive coaches (but more of that later!).

Type theory helps us to understand and work with our preferences, in order that we may fundamentally understand who we are and what unique ingredients we bring to our daily interactions with others. This self-awareness is a crucial component to leadership development, where a confusing plethora of models, formulas and inspirational anecdotal accounts makes it confusing for the aspiring leader to discern which approach they should take. The quest for some perfect style of leadership is an admirable but futile ambition and I frequently find myself drawing upon Type theory to explain and reassure that there are many different ways to achieve effective leadership and that none of them require a programme in personality transformation.

As coaches, our role is to help people to build their leadership capability on a firm foundation of self-awareness and to facilitate their conscious choice about being the best leader that they can be, rather than the one that that they think that they ought to be. These beliefs about leadership may stem from some role model that they are copying, or from the comforting formulaic principles espoused by business schools and consultants like myself! In the midst of all of this chatter, it is understandably easy for people to lose sight of what their natural preferences are and which style of leadership may be most productive for them. The essence of leadership coaching is to work with people to help them find their strengths and to explore how these can be applied in a positive and constructive manner. But Type theory tells us that there are aspects of our personality which are not obviously positive strengths – let's face it, there are negative, dysfunctional, unhelpful and sometimes scary aspects of ourselves that we would much rather not talk about! This chapter aims to illustrate the benefits of looking at both sides of our personality – in short, our bright side and dark side, and offer some suggestions and reassurance as to how we might do both. I hope that executive coaches will find some ideas on how they can integrate Type into their work, and I'll also provide suggestions on how we can all use Type for our own self-development.

### Why look at both the bright and dark sides?

It shouldn't be hard to define and identify our bright side – that aspect of our personality that we show when we feel at our comfortable best ,and that we can consciously control. One challenge here though is that we may not be so clear about what this is and therefore find it rather difficult to consciously control. Perhaps we have been investing a lot of energy in adapting our behaviours to meet the expectations of others, either in a professional or family context, and have become confused about what our natural preferred style is. For example, a desire to please others by demonstrating an organised and structured approach may be inhibiting a natural preference for spontaneity and adaptability. By contrast, our dark side contains negative qualities and dysfunctional tendencies about which we are either less conscious or completely unaware. Should we stumble across them or find ourselves confronted by them, we are far less comfortable in their presence, or even embarrassed or ashamed of them. Understandably we are less likely to welcome the opportunity to reveal the contents of these murky depths, although they may make their presence felt at times of stress and we generally become better acquainted with them as we mature. On the other hand, our dark side may not necessarily be all bad, but could equally be a place of hidden treasures, a store of hitherto untapped potential that we are in danger of denying ourselves access to if we never go searching of it. For example, in my case, my preference for deep reflection can sometimes inhibit the 'just do it' experiential part of me from ever emerging, but when I deliberately allow the unleashing of that aspect of me then the results can be quite invigorating! If we are prepared to look at both our bright and dark sides, then we are more likely to achieve some integration between the conscious and unconscious parts of our psyche, helping us to find a greater sense of equilibrium. For leaders wishing to discover and nurture their authentic style, this kind of work can prove invaluable, as it will enable them to work comfortably with their natural style but also adapt more easily to those environments that require a different approach.

The following cases will hopefully illustrate how a leadership coach can work with people to both help them fully realise the capacity of their bright side and tap into the relatively unexplored opportunities that reside in their dark side. The role of the coach is to act as a mirror – reflecting back the image of the bright side with as much clarity and accuracy as possible, but also bouncing back the fainter glimmers that emerge from the darker side – guiding the person in their discovery.

The source of the light, in both cases, must come from the individual coachee – they are responsible for picking up the torch. It is not the role of the coach to lead this exploration or to indulge in some psychotherapeutic excavation. These examples come from my personal experience of coaching leaders in a range of situations – some of them from observing people in group exercises during intensive leadership development programmes and others from one-to-one coaching assignments. Listening to or watching leaders in these circumstances can be a labour of joy or frustration. To see and hear people absolutely in their element by leveraging their natural preferences is inspirational – whether it is the SJ (introverted Sensing) Type recalling and managing vast amounts of data, or the Intuitive who creates a compelling vision for the future of their organisation – a preference that is realised and consciously deployed is impactful. Of course, it is not possible to predict that the outcomes will be effective leadership – we are only talking here about preferences rather than skill and the impact will always be contingent upon the context. But through the conscious realisation of their preferences, leaders will be better placed to learn about what works for them, in what circumstances and how they need to adapt where necessary. On the other hand, when leaders are either not fully utilising their natural gifts or keep tripping over some aspect of themselves that they would rather deny the existence of than confront, I share their sense of frustration and curiosity about why this keeps happening!

### When your bright side isn't bright enough

Strange as it may sound, some people are not sufficiently acquainted with their bright side, or simply do not trust it to serve them well enough in their leadership challenges. For example, Julie (ENFP) displayed little of the typical energy, enthusiasm or support to people that many with her preferences do, but instead attempted to lead a team through a complex group exercise by emphasising structure, objectivity and close attention to detail. As this was acting outside of her natural preferences, it took extra energy from her and the result felt, to myself looking on and to her team mates in the exercise, a little laboured. Her team initially co-operated but found themselves getting bogged down in the repetitive re-clarifying of agenda items and exasperated that there was no unifying vision or strategy for their collective actions. Feeling and perhaps sharing their welling frustration, Julie suddenly snapped into her default mode and began articulating the vision and values that she held for herself and the future of the team – and in that moment the energy in the room changed. People suddenly felt a sense of purpose and conviction in Julie that mobilised their resources and motivated them to apply themselves to their individual and collective tasks.

When I discussed this with her later, Julie acknowledged that she had been trying to act as the kind of 'organised leader' that she felt that she ought to be, fearing that her own preferences might be perceived as a bit 'woolly'. Julie, like many of us, was confusing style of approach with outcomes – of course nobody wants confusion or vagueness and attention to detail and structure are important, but these outcomes can be achieved by any number of different approaches, and the one that comes naturally is the one that is most likely to have the greatest energy behind it. When we inject energy into a system, such as a team of people, we enable it to mobilise the resources that it has and respond to its challenges. An analogy is an engine, where a complex system of interconnected parts cannot function at all without the provision of some source of energy or fuel. Julie could mobilise and enable the team as a whole to manage the detail and structure through the natural flow of her preference, injecting a sense of purpose and mission that provided a guiding framework.

As the coach working with Julie's team, it was important for me to be aware of my own level of energy, commitment and clarity that I felt as I observed the team, and to notice the impact of Julie's behaviour on others. The contrasting impact between the two styles that Julie had displayed was so striking, that it took only a gentle invitation to her to look at herself and notice which behaviour had been most effective for her. Her bright side of Intuition and Feeling had been supressed by her early attempts to adopt a more Sensing and Thinking style and apply this to detailed planning and organising. When she saw the results of unleashing the force of her natural preferences, Julie gained far more confidence in her ability to lead a team, whatever the circumstances, and with this renewed confidence she found it much easier to deal with the demands of structure and detail as well.

In summary, my role as a coach here was to invite Julie to look in the mirror and see the true image of who she really was, and not the image of the leader that she felt that she ought to be. Listening out for expressions like "I ought to ..." or "I should be ..." is essential for a coach wishing to help people expose and then challenge the validity of their assumptions about what 'good leadership' looks like. Effective leadership takes many different forms and we may be undervaluing our naturally gifted style by trying to conform to some perceived stereotype.

## When your bright side is hidden – the challenge for Introverts

The challenge of under-utilising their bright side is particularly prevalent amongst Introverts, whose brightest side is, by definition, somewhat hidden from the outside world. Mark (INFP), like many Introverts, was quite aware that he appeared relatively quiet in meetings, as his internal Feeling function was hard at work processing issues against his internal set of values. At the same time, he appreciated that it was important for him to be seen as being present during these meetings and making contributions to his colleagues, particularly as he had recently been promoted to a higher profile position where there were significant expectations of him to perform. But, as much as he knew this, flexing his behaviour out if his habitual silence proved difficult and stressful. In our coaching session Mark identified that he was comfortable in taking to the stage and doing the "Extraverted stuff" when formally invited to do so and when he felt that he was confident with his level of expertise in the subject matter. So, to him, it felt like his bright side was the Extraverted one that could go out and perform to the group, leaving the shy and timid side cursing and regretting his own inaction. The resulting tension between the two of these components of his personality was creating in Mark an anxiety –

although he was clear that his preference was for Introversion, he was uncertain and distrustful of the contribution that his supposed bright side could make. It just didn't feel that bright to him!

As in any tense relationship, resolution required the two parties to come together for a dialogue about their needs and wants. In coaching, an effective medium for this is a chair exercise, whereby the two sides of Mark (or 'sub-personalities') are given a voice from their own chair and allowed to question and debate with each other (although both of the characters are played by Mark as he moves from one chair to another). The Extraverted Mark explained how he felt embarrassed by the lack of presence of his Introverted counterpart, and that in meetings he would psychologically move alongside the other members of the group to look on his Introverted self with disappointment and disdain. However, the Introverted Mark was not going to accept this mocking, asserting that he did have an important role to play and that there were certain types of meetings where his quiet reflective approach was more productive. Instead of allowing them to argue over who was right or wrong, I encouraged them to agree some 'rules of engagement' about who should be appointed for specific tasks. The resulting agreement gave both of these sub-personalities a new legitimacy and removed the tension between them. As a result of lifting this tension, Mark felt that he could more easily switch between the two modes – comfortably and confidently demanding the space to express the thoughtful outputs of his Introverted bright side when he felt that he needed to, and in other situations sending out the Extravert when it was 'show time' for his capabilities. Crucial to the effective management of this 'team Mark' approach, was the appointment of a third person, 'Clarity Mark', whose role it was to be the judge of what the situation required and to appoint the right Mark for the job!

As a coach, my role with Mark was to pick up the tension and anxiety that he was feeling and to provide a framework for him to explore this. The concept of sub-personalities is particularly compatible with Type theory because it allows an exploration of how these different dimensions of our personality are expressed and the interplay between them. By following the naturally emerging flow of energy and emotion during the exercise, Mark was able to navigate a way through his dilemma and find a practical resolution.

## Tips and ideas for developing the bright side

As a coach:

- Notice the energy flow in people and the impact that it has on you. When the bright side is talking there will generally be a sparkle in their eye and a conviction in their tone.
- Encourage people to notice this energy in themselves and the impact that they have on others.
- If the bright side is being hidden or frightened away to hide in the background, it could be due some tension created by the expectations of others. These others could be other people or different parts of our own personality. In either case, get the conflicting components into a dialogue explore how the restrictions on the bright side can be lifted and its legitimacy reinforced.

## For our self-development:

- Notice your own energy flow and the impact on others around you.
- If you are an Introvert, don't devalue the work that you do inside your head but assert your right for attention when you are ready to share the results.
- Remember that effective leadership can be achieved in different ways. Focus on the outcomes and discover your preferred way of achieving them, rather than following a stereotype.

## The dark side

The dark side, by definition, is hidden from ourselves, in that it is an aspect of our personality that is less conscious and accessible than our bright side. We may become acquainted with it from time to time, perhaps when we are stressed and under pressure or, as Jung believed, during our dreams. The expression 'in the grip' (of our inferior function or lesser used part of our Type) refers to the phenomenon of a sudden appearance of our dark side, often resulting in a transformation in our personality. To ourselves and onlookers, this may look like an unfamiliar version of us that may be rather awkward or dysfunctional. Whilst the appearance of our dark side during an 'in the grip' episode may be unwelcome and alarming, it is possible for us to become acquainted with our darker aspects in a more deliberate and constructive manner, so we can enjoy a relatively harmonious and productive relationship with it. In other words, we can take possession of our dark side instead of it possessing us!

As a coach, my role is to support my clients in that exploration of the dark side, should they feel sufficient curiosity to do so. The dark side will frequently make its presence felt during a coaching conversation, particularly when our clients become more anxious and their normal steady state becomes challenged. Their communication may become less lucid, more hesitant with a drop or change in energy. At this point, both coach and client need gather some courage, with the client picking up their torch, the coach reflecting back the images that appear and together embarking on the exploration. Whilst there are no guaranteed destinations of enlightenment to reward this courage, the journey can provide insights into hitherto undiscovered capabilities that we have rarely accessed or utilised.

## A confrontational approach

Steve was an ENTJ engineer, project managing a large scale and complex infrastructure scheme. At his best, Steve was comfortable in solving problems, setting long-term goals and marshalling the resources to achieve his targets. Like many of his Type, Steve also demonstrated a high level of concern for his own level of competency and would relish taking on a challenge to prove to himself his capability. However, under the pressure of constantly moving deadlines and priorities, he would start to examine his own ability to cope and question the capability of others around him. Despite feeling that he was a competent leader of his team, Steve would frequently ask his manager for guidance and direction on how he could improve his effectiveness. He also reported that during meetings with his peers he often felt criticised and that he perceived some their 'attacks' as arrogant and belittling of him. During a coaching session, Steve and I were role-playing a conversation that he intended to have with his boss, the objective of which was to obtain some strategic guidance and, as usual, some feedback on how he was performing in his leadership of the project. Instinctively, I found myself responding in a provocative, almost taunting mode, saying "Why don't you show me some leadership instead of asking me to for guidance and feedback! I feel unsure about what it is that you want from me." There was a long pause and for a few moments Steve appeared quite troubled. When he spoke he said that he felt unappreciated and unwanted by his boss, but he began to see that it was a good working relationship with him that wanted to build, and not just affirmation of his competency.

Steve's dark side includes aspects of the subjective Feeling preference, the opposite of his more accustomed and comfortable, objective Thinking preference. One possible manifestation of this dark side is a hypersensitivity towards his own emotional state, resulting in him feeling victimised and unappreciated. By surfacing this feeling, Steve could become more consciously aware of this under-utilised facet of his personality – namely his capacity to gauge his self-esteem not just by his competence, but by the strength of his relationships. He then identified other ways by which he could explore and develop the relationship with his boss. For example, he decided to focus more attention on exploring his boss's personal perspective of the project as a whole and not just the objective evaluation of achievements and deadlines. Steve also explored ways to examine his own emotional state, for example, by pausing to ask himself "what am I feeling now?" and "is this how I want to be feeling?", and began to discover that this hitherto considered 'irrational' side, could provide him with some helpful, complimentary perspectives. He also began to recognise that the confrontation and arrogance that he perceived to be directed towards him by his colleagues, could be a projection of his own self-critical thoughts. Projection is just one defence mechanism that our minds can deploy when we experience thoughts or feelings that are uncomfortable to us. Instead of saying to ourselves, "I am a failure", we may attribute these thoughts to others and convert it to "they think I am a failure".

Steve was, therefore, hearing in their words the anxieties that he felt about his own competence. He explored how he could take ownership of these concerns and deal with them himself, starting by being a little kinder and more forgiving of himself when he felt the pressure to perform.

As a coach, my role with Steve was to confront him with a response to something that I detected in the space between us, but which was not being openly articulated. To me it felt like a sensitivity and neediness within him which I instinctively reacted to with my confrontational response. Now let's leave aside the issue of how that response was shaped by my own 'stuff' (which, of course, it would be) or whether this was the right or wrong thing to say. The point is that I risked acting on some instinctive feeling that changed the energy and focus between us. The light was now being reflected back on to Steve and illuminating something that he sensed was there, but was unaccustomed to giving much attention to. The silence and space that I then allowed him enabled Steve to discover some value in working with his newly surfaced darker side.

### The use of humour – taking issues to the absurd

Another tactic to provoke the dark side to come out of its hiding place is through humour. When we exaggerate our fears to point where they appear absurd we can often create some psychological distance from ourselves, allowing us to look and laugh at ourselves in order to gain a more constructive perspective. By taking ourselves so seriously we begin to believe our own internal propaganda about the people that we feel we ought to be and find it harder to look at and accept the true image in the mirror. . Much of the conventional coaching approaches draw upon the world of positive psychology, encouraging clients to visualise positive outcomes and realise the strengths that they can draw upon to achieve their goals. But what happens if we playfully encourage our clients to contemplate the absolute opposite, that is, the complete and utter failure to achieve their goals? And instead looking at strengths, let's dredge up all of those odious qualities which they would rather stay hidden, but which they suspect may be contributing towards their downfall?

For example, John (ISTJ) could usually rely upon his SJ (introverted Sensing) to help to bring an order and efficiency to the organisation of data and tasks. As the pressure on his role grew, it became increasingly necessary for him to delegate more tasks to other members of his team, a fact that was obvious to John's rational mind but which was proving difficult for him to implement in practice. Instead, he would take on more and more responsibility without complaint and attempt to complete the tasks to his own high standards by working longer hours. John was effectively locked into a system of thinking that perfectly maintained this awful status quo, by holding onto the contradictory beliefs that delegation was the right thing to do, but also that he was indispensable because his own standards of work could not be achieved by anyone else!

Judging that our coaching relationship was secure enough to engage a more playful approach, I invited John to imagine that he had utterly failed to achieve his goal and describe to me the horrible consequences. The following is a synopsis of just one part of our conversation – there were many more exchanges and many more laughs than outlined below:

John: "Well, if I don't maintain my high standards, then there would be serious consequences for me and the organisation."
Coach: "And what might they be?"
John: "The project would overrun and exceed its budget and I would be held responsible."
Coach: "This is great – but let's keep working at this catastrophe because I'm sure that things could get a lot worse than that, couldn't they?"
John: "Ultimately I could lose my job ... my career would be in ruins ... I could be out on the street without a home."
Coach: "Excellent! This sounds like a really useful catastrophe for us to work on. So how can we make it happen? How realistic does this scenario feel to you?"
John: "Well, when I look at it like that, then I guess that I may be guilty of exaggerating a little – to get from making a few mistakes to being out on the street is a bit of a leap!"

Coach "Well I'm sure that if you put your mind to it John, you could achieve it! But it does seem a bit of a stretch doesn't it! Now assuming that you have been successful in bringing about this catastrophe, in what ways might you have contributed towards this scenario?"

John: "It sounds like I am losing a sense of perspective; getting too caught up in the detail and not stepping back to look at the bigger picture and insisting that my perfectionism is the only thing that counts around here."

Coach: "Does it feel frightening to look at that bigger picture at the expense of the dealing with the detail?"

John: "Yes it does! But, then again, I can see some situations where it would be quite helpful to take that approach,"

John was beginning to get more familiarity with his darker Intuitive side and began to see that this was not necessarily the frightening beast that he imagined when he first contemplated the possibility of letting slip his attention to detail. Instead, he saw that it could be used as a useful ally to him if he allowed himself to befriend this side of himself and work together with it constructively. For example, John began to place more trust in his capability to articulate a vision for his team and to accept that others may have different perspectives and capabilities to himself. He began to find the prospect of coaching others to discover their own way of finding solutions to problems as a far more interesting prospect.

As a coach, my role here was to enable John to question his serious and earnest appraisal of the situation, provoking him to re-evaluate his underlying assumption that there was no alternative but to carry on with his perfectionist ways and to keep on doing what had always worked for him in the past. The wisdom of this playful approach is for every coach to decide, based upon the quality of their relationship with the coachee. If a client is deeply fearful of the situation then they may not find such an approach to be appealing or useful, but, in my experience, such cases are in the minority.

## Tips and ideas for coaching the dark side

As a coach:

- Just as in coaching for the bright side, notice the person's energy flow and the impact that it has on you as a coach. When people begin to encounter their dark side there can be a lowering of the energy or a cautiousness in their approach. Reflect back what you sense and encourage your client to keep exploring what it is that they are experiencing.
- Our instinctive responses to our coachees may not be comfortable when they are exploring their dark side, but take courage and share your insights when you sense that they may help.
- Sometimes you may find a provocative or playful approach helps to reflect some light and draw their attention to an un-explored aspect of their personality.

For our self-development:

- Study your own response to stress. What aspects of your personality come out and how could you use them more constructively?
- Don't take yourself too seriously! Humour and playfulness can be an effective way to break down some of the barriers that we put in place to protect ourselves from the fear of the unknown.
- Be courageous. Exploring our dark side can be frightening but the journey can lead us to a deeper sense of wholeness and completeness.

I began this chapter with an appeal to look at the world not just through the lens of 'glass half full' or 'glass half empty', but to do both. I hope that my accounts of experiences of working with people in leadership development have demonstrated the value of helping them to realise their potential by drawing upon their unique combination of capabilities from both their bright and dark sides. I believe that they discover a greater range of effective leadership styles and are seen as being more authentic to those around them. As coaches, we should do the same work on ourselves, which brings me back to that moment when

I dropped my trousers in front of an audience. As mentioned earlier, my own reflective style can sometimes inhibit a more experiential approach – that rash "to hell with it; let's feel the fear and do it anyway!" voice is definitely from a dangerous dark side beast, lurking in the cellar of my mind! So what better way to give it some 'exposure' than by dropping my trousers mid-way through a presentation on, well, you might have guessed, 'The dark side of coaching'! Funnily enough (and there were as many laughs as there were screams of embarrassment), the experience was far more enlightening than 'endarkening'! If I can survive that, then a whole new world of experiential approaches to learning has definitely opened up, and I don't have to drop my trousers to enjoy them!

# :: Acknowledgements ::

There are a great many people without whom this book wouldn't have happened. First of course are the authors who have all taken time out of running their businesses to put their chapters together, under very tight deadlines. Hazel was also hugely helpful in providing advice and reviews, Linn was, as in all things, my partner in this project. Whilst Tegan and Maya brought encouragement and pictures to keep us all going.

Then I must thank Jenny Collins, our copy editor for ensuring that all our varied chapters can be read by other people, without losing what each of the authors has brought. Christian Bilbow provided the great, eye-catching cover and Sarah for her work putting together the layout.

Printed in Great Britain
by Amazon.co.uk, Ltd.,
Marston Gate.

9972435R00118